INCARNATION

New Century Theology

Other books in this series include:

INCARNATION

Gerald O'Collins

New Century Theology

continuum
LONDON • NEW YORK

CONTINUUM
The Tower Building, 11 York Road, London SE1 7NX
370 Lexington Avenue, New York NY 10017-6503

www.continuumbooks.com

First published 2002

British Library Cataloguing-in-Publication Data
A catalogue record for this book is available from the British Library.

ISBN: 0-8264-5535-2

Typeset by Kenneth Burnley, Wirral, Cheshire
Printed and bound in Great Britain by The Cromwell Press, Trowbridge,
Wiltshire

Contents

For Stephen Davis, Daniel Kendall,
and all the participants in the New York 'Summits'

Introduction

Modern astronomy has shown how our universe is too big for thinking. There are around 100,000 million galaxies in the universe, each containing about 100,000 million stars. If every human being on the face of the earth started counting the stars at the rate of five per second, it would take 10,000 years to complete the tally. In our gigantic universe so much is uncountable, unknowable, or only dimly understood.

The mind-blowing discoveries of modern astronomy and physics hint at the way God is too big for thinking. Nevertheless, from the start of Christianity, Justin Martyr (d. *c.* 165), Irenaeus (d. *c.* 200), Tertullian (d. *c.* 225), Origen (d. *c.* 254), Athanasius of Alexandria (d. 373), Gregory of Nazianzus (d. 389/90) and their colleagues and successors felt compelled to reflect on the divine mystery and delve, in particular, into the central truth of the Word of God 'becoming flesh and dwelling among us' (John 1.14).

Our questions and conclusions should never pretend to master the truth of the incarnation. They remain part of the triple homage owed to God: the homage of our intellect and its exploration of truth; that of faithful discipleship in the service of love, justice, and the common good; that of our worship in praise of the divine benevolence and glorious beauty. Faced with the 'frightening and fascinating' self-revelation of God in Jesus Christ, we approach this awesome mystery with our minds on stretch, our hands at work and our hearts at prayer. What questions about the incarnation can attract the homage of our intellect, and at least indirectly improve our discipleship and inspire our worship?

Chapter 1 will explore the primary meaning of incarnation faith. Does it propose a particular, in fact a unique and uniquely significant, event, an occurrence that is strictly the only one of its kind? Or are G. W. F. Hegel, D. F. Strauss, Joseph Campbell, John Hick and others right in expounding (albeit in various ways and for different reasons) the incarnation as a *general* truth about the human condition – a possibility for any generous and Spirit-filled person? Here we face also the closely related question: is faith in the incarnation peculiar to Christianity? Or is a truly similar faith found in the Srivaishnava tradition of Hinduism, which proposes ten primary 'avatars' or 'descents' of God to earth?

Chapter 2 will look backwards both to explore possible 'precedents' for the incarnation in Jewish faith and to reflect on the personal pre-existence of the divine Word or Wisdom who was to become flesh. Exploring what came 'before' the incarnation will also include reflection on the function of the not-yet-incarnate Word in the creation and in the history of the world.

Chapter 3 will look forward from the incarnation to what follows in the life, death and resurrection of Jesus, with the coming of the Holy Spirit, and the eventual transformation of humanity and the world at the end of time. How can one hold together that whole story from the Baby in Bethlehem to the coming of 'the new heaven' and 'the new earth'?

Chapter 4 faces the mysterious paradox of the incarnation: one and the same individual being both divinely infinite and humanly finite. Can one individual possess simultaneously all the necessary divine and human characteristics?

Chapter 5 reflects on the self-limitation that the incarnation involved. Did the startling 'self-emptying' invoked by St Paul (Philippians 2.7) entail, for instance, that God the Son became, at least for a time, bereft of his divine powers?

Chapter 6 explores the classical teaching and terminology of the Council of Chalcedon (451): one (divine) person 'in' two natures. Are that teaching and the terms in which it was expressed still viable, and should it continue to guide our talk about Jesus Christ? How might that teaching allow us to follow ancient Christian writers, Martin Luther and others in confessing that 'God who exists from all eternity died for us on the cross'?

Chapter 7 moves on to some difficult implications of the Chalcedonian teaching: the incarnate Son of God possessed and possesses a human mind and will, along with his divine mind and will. How might we go even a short distance in envisaging the scope of his human knowledge and the connection between his human and divine minds? Granted that his human will let him become subject to temptation, what should we say about Christ's sinlessness? Is it incoherent to envisage someone who is both liable to be tempted and yet incapable of sinning?

Chapter 8 examines the mode of unity enacted in the incarnation. Is the union it entails between being human and being divine something like the union between body and soul?

According to the Gospels of Matthew and Luke, the virginal conception was the historical way the incarnation actually took place. Chapter 9 asks: is the virginal conception still historically defensible? If so, what might it mean for the whole story of human salvation through the incarnate Son of God?

Chapter 10 will look at the redeeming love expressed and deployed in the incarnation. An adequate view of the incarnation allows one to glimpse the power of God's saving love for human beings and their world.

Chapter 11 will take up the issue of credibility. Can faith in something so extraordinary as the incarnation of the pre-existent Son of God enjoy some degree of plausibility? How far can a case be made in support of the incarnation?

Chapter 12 will highlight and synthesize what seem to be the better insights that have emerged in this study of the incarnation.

I am very grateful to Robin Baird-Smith for encouraging me to write this book, as well as to the members of one graduate course and two graduate seminars at the Gregorian University for their valuable contributions to my thinking about the incarnation. Yet I do not want to clutter the book with too many 'scholarly' notes and bibliography; that academic apparatus will be kept down to a minimum. With much affection and gratitude I dedicate this book to Steve Davis, Dan Kendall and the other scholars who shared in our wonderful Easter meetings at St Joseph's Seminary, Dunwoodie (Yonkers, New York): the Resurrection Summit (1996), the Trinity Summit (1998) and the Incarnation Summit (2000).

GERALD O'COLLINS
Gregorian University, Rome
October 2001

Abbreviations

d.   died (with date)

DH   H. Denzinger and P. Hünermann (eds), *Enchiridion Symbolorum, Definitionum et Declarationum* etc., 37 ed. (Freiburg: Herder, 1991)

LXX   Septuagint

ND   J. Neuner and J. Dupuis (eds), *The Christian Faith*, 7 ed. (Bangalore: Theological Publications in India, 2001)

NT   New Testament

OT   Old Testament

ST   Thomas Aquinas, *Summa Theologiae*

1

The Meaning of 'Incarnation'

He was manifested in the flesh, vindicated by the
Spirit, appeared to angels, proclaimed among the
nations, believed in throughout the world, taken up to
glory. (1 Timothy 3.16)

In the face of this mysterious reality [the incarnation],
either we could talk for ever, or we could find ourselves
wordless. (Peter Steele, *On Saying Yes,* unpublished
sermon)

Before patiently examining different questions raised by
belief in the incarnation, we need to clarify at the outset the
way this book will use 'incarnation'.

The primary meaning

The earliest sense of the English word 'incarnation', created
by merely adding an 'n' to the original Latin *incarnatio*, still
remains its primary or literal meaning: the Word or Son of
God was 'made flesh' or 'in-carnated' by assuming a complete
human nature and not simply an external bodily form. At a
certain point in human history God acted in a special, in fact
unique, way through the once-and-for-all 'sending' or 'coming'
of his Son. The primary meaning is the 'classical' doctrine: the
eternal Son of God took flesh from his human mother; hence

the person known as Jesus of Nazareth was and is at once
fully human and truly divine; his history is the 'enfleshed'
story of the Son of God, and no 'mere' theophany or transitory
appearance of God.

Three outstanding theologians of the New Testament (here-
after NT) use different idioms to witness to the incarnation
that initiated and underpinned the whole story of Jesus. The
earliest Christian writer, St Paul, turned to hymnic language
and wrote of One who was 'in the form of God' but 'did not
think his equality with God a thing to be exploited' for his own
advantage. Rather he 'emptied himself' by assuming 'the form
of a slave', became like us, and 'was revealed' in the human
condition (Philippians 2.6–7). Here the humble initiative of
the Son is to the fore: in the incarnation he 'took on the form of
a slave' and would end his human life on a cross.

The anonymous author of the Letter to the Hebrews,
writing perhaps ten years later, presented the incarnation as
the decisive climax of a divine preparation that had taken
centuries of Jewish history:

> In many and varied ways God spoke long ago to our
> forefathers through the prophets. But in these last days
> he has spoken to us through a Son, whom he has
> appointed the heir of all things; and through him he
> created the world.
>
> He is the reflection of God's glory and the stamp of
> God's very being, and he supports all things by his word
> of power. After he had made purification for sins, he
> took his place at the right hand of the Majesty on high.
> (Hebrews 1.1–3)

This stately opening to Hebrews, more than the Letter to the
Philippians, describes what the Son is like – as 'the reflection
of God's glory and the stamp of God's very being'. It proclaims
the Son's role in creation, and puts his incarnation in context

by evoking Jewish history through a series of contrasts. It is the same God who has spoken and speaks now, but what was said 'long ago' to 'our forefathers' and 'through the prophets' is contrasted with what has been personally said 'in these last days' 'to us' and 'through the Son'. The 'many and varied ways' of earlier divine revelation have reached their decisive and unified completion in the revelation of the incarnate Son who is the perfect counterpart of God the Father. After purifying human sins through his sacrificial death and resurrection, the Son has taken his place for ever at God's right hand as the eternal high priest – a theme to be developed extensively in later chapters of Hebrews. Thus the opening verses of Hebrews, unlike Paul in Philippians, indicate the revealing and saving thrust of the incarnation. Through the incarnate son, God has spoken to us (= revelation) and purified our sins (= salvation).

When presenting his classic account of the incarnation, the author of John's Gospel spells out even more Jewish history and creation, but reverses the order which we find in the opening verses of Hebrews. He recalls by name (and not simply in general by speaking of 'forefathers' and 'prophets') the role of John the Baptist and then of Moses (John 1.6–8, 15, 17), but only after announcing that the whole of creation has come into being through the divine Word (John 1.3; see also 1.10). By evoking at greater length creation and then history, John's prologue fashions the setting for the majestic proclamation: 'the Word became flesh and made his home among us; and we saw his glory, the glory of the Father's only-begotten Son' (John 1.14). The incarnation forms the once-and-for-all, supremely decisive moment in God's saving and revealing dealings (of 'life' and 'light', respectively) with the Jewish people, with all people (John 1.9, 12–13), and with the whole cosmos. God is now personally disclosed in one, and only one, individual, born at a specific time (normally reckoned as around 5 BC) to grow up in a particular place, Nazareth (John 1.45–6).

This primary meaning of 'incarnation', attested by Paul, the Letter to the Hebrews, and John, makes faith in the incarnate Son of God scandalously particular and particularly scandalous. Why did such an incarnation not occur 300 years earlier, around the time of Alexander the Great, and in a different country: for example, in Greece or India? Or why didn't it take place 2,000 years later, for instance, in modern Korea? And then why was the Word of God incarnated in a Jewish male and not, let us say, in a Melanesian female? These and similar questions will return again and again in this book, surfacing, for example, when we face the issue of the believability of mainline Christian faith in Jesus as the once-and-for-all incarnation of God the Son. At this point I am concerned simply with clarifying the primary meaning of incarnation, the event which not only marks for ever the beginning of the Christian era but also forms *the* watershed in the history of humanity and the created cosmos. Let me name this primary meaning as meaning (A).

Extended usage

Before facing some modern challenges to what has been sketched as the primary meaning of 'incarnation', we should recall certain extended usages of incarnation language that emerged centuries ago. This language was applied to those who strikingly 'embody' some quality, be it good or evil. Thus the wicked Iago in Shakespeare's *Othello* could be described as 'the devil incarnate'. Recently a reviewer of J. K. Rowling's *Harry Potter and the Goblet of Fire* declared that Voldemort, the arch baddie of earlier Harry Potter books, is now revealed as 'an incarnation of supreme evil' (*The Tablet*, 5 August 2000). In a positive way, a gracious, warm-hearted person might be called 'the very incarnation of affability'. Some speak of Andy Warhol, the living embodiment of pop art, as having 'incarnated' the spirit of postmodernism.

In all these cases, talk of 'incarnation' is extended to a good or bad quality or attribute dramatically embodied in some person's character or work. It is never a question, as in the primary sense, of a heavenly person, and not merely a quality, being 'enfleshed' in a human being. Unless one wants to understand Iago as Satan himself in person, the primary and the extended cases of incarnation language differ from each other inasmuch as persons differ from qualities or attributes. Let me name this extended usage meaning (B).

A general truth?

At least from the nineteenth century, some Christians or post-Christians have taken (or should one say reduced?) 'incarnation' to mean some general truth about the human condition. So far from limiting it to a unique case, that of the Son of God 'become flesh' 2,000 years ago, they interpret incarnation as a possibility for all men and women, or at least for all human beings open to their ultimate potential. Let us look at G. W. F. Hegel (1770–1831), D. F. Strauss (1808–74), D. H. Lawrence (1885–1930), Joseph Campbell (1904–87) and John Hick (b. 1922), who in different ways and, often, for somewhat different reasons, propose 'incarnation' as such a general possibility.

Thus Hegel interpreted the incarnation in a universal way (as God appearing in every rational, human being) rather than in terms of an individual and even unique event of incarnation (as the Son of God's once-and-for-all incarnation in a particular man). Hegel understood incarnation to be a general truth about the human condition – namely, the highest form of religious 'representation' or 'image' that synthesizes the 'contradictions' between the human and the divine. This universal interpretation of the incarnation followed from Hegel's philosophy of the human individual being the appearance of the divine essence, and of God 'appearing' as every instance of universal, human thinking. In this way Hegel could extend to all human beings the truth of the divine–human unity found in the incarnation.[1]

Deeply influenced by Hegel and taking his thought further, Strauss argued that the idea of 'God–manhood' or the unity of divine and human natures cannot be restricted to a single exemplar (Jesus) but is realized in 'the whole race of mankind'. So far from the 'incarnation of God' being 'limited to a particular point in time', it is an idea that exists in the entire reality of humanity itself. Each individual may participate 'in the divinely human life of the species'. Thus, for Strauss, the finite and infinite are unified collectively or in all humanity. One might sum up Strauss' view as 'the truth of the incarnation is found in the whole'.[2]

In his poem 'The Body of God' Lawrence celebrated 'any lovely and generous woman' and 'any clear and fearless man' as 'god, very god'. One can hear and see the incarnation of beauty when men sing their songs and women brush their hair in the bright sun. Such women and men, even more than beautiful carnations, poppies and flying fish, incarnate the divine, above all by showing themselves sexually liberated – lovely women being generous with their sexual favours and men being clear and fearless in their passionate overtures and 'urge' to find the female body. Lawrence names only three lovely persons who as 'god' have 'come to pass': the legendary Helen of Troy who abandoned her husband to join Paris and so trigger off the Trojan War; the refined but highly promiscuous French courtesan Ninon de l'Enclos (1620–1705); and Jesus himself. One must be grateful that, at least in this poem, Lawrence did not attribute to Jesus the sexual activities found in Lawrence's posthumous novella, *The Man Who Died*. The poem exemplifies that decadent or even perverse use of Christian language and symbols that angered Lawrence's contemporary, T. S. Eliot (1888–1965). It is worth quoting the poem in full.

God is the great urge that has not yet found a body
but urges towards incarnation with the great creative
    urge.
And becomes at last a clove carnation: lo! that is god!
and becomes at last Helen, or Ninon: any lovely and
    generous woman
at her best and her most beautiful, being god, made
    manifest,
and clear and fearless man being god, very god.
There is no god
apart from poppies and the flying fish,
men singing songs, and women brushing their hair in
    the sun.
The lovely things are god that has come to pass,
    like Jesus came.
The rest, the undiscoverable is the demiurge.

In his best-seller, *The Hero with a Thousand Faces* (original edition 1949), Joseph Campbell took Jesus to be a universal hero like Gautama Buddha or Mohammed, one who brings 'a message for the entire world'. Repeatedly playing down the historical diversities and differences, Campbell found a single pattern underlying various myths and legends of humanity: 'the hero as the incarnation of God is himself the navel of the world, the umbilical point through which the energies of eternity break into time'. The archetypal hero directs each of us to our 'immanent divinity'. The 'divine being' reveals 'the omnipotent Self, which dwells within us all'. The lesson for everyone is: 'Know this and be God.' Campbell flatteringly invited us to take up our hero-task and answer the call of 'the inexhaustible and multifariously wonderful divine existence that is the life in all of us'.[3] We too can enjoy a splendid triumph of the human spirit by letting our immanent divinity emerge and come into its own.

Hegel's philosophy pushed Strauss into radically reinterpreting 'incarnation'. Lawrence and Campbell had their own literary and mythological agenda, respectively. All four stretch the definition of the incarnation to an extreme.

Such stretching of the definition continues, albeit for somewhat different motives. Recent revisionists are often driven by the conviction that the classic doctrine of incarnation, meaning (A), inevitably entails unacceptable religious exclusivism, an arrogant claim that, having been founded by the incarnate Son of God, Christianity is superior and unique. These two intertwined claims must be avoided at all costs if we are going to promote real inter-religious dialogue and peace. Hence meaning (A) is suppressed and some form of meaning (B) takes over: 'incarnation' means embodying some highly desirable religious quality.

Thus for John Hick, Jesus 'embodied, or incarnated, the ideal of human life lived in faithful response to God'. Hick describes Jesus accordingly: he 'embodied a love which is a [not the!] human reflection of the divine love'.[4] Hick has developed a view in which Jesus is a guru, rather than being a (still less *the*) saviour; he is a great religious teacher and an outstanding spiritual guide along with others. The 'ultimate transcendent Reality which is the source and ground of everything', Hick writes, 'is reflected ("incarnated") in human terms in the lives of the world's great spiritual leaders'.[5] In Hick's view, Jesus differs from other Spirit-filled or saintly persons only in degree and not in kind. At best Jesus is merely the highest human example of someone open to and utterly motivated by the divine spirit. In a 'Letter to the Editors: Incarnation' Hick endorsed this line of argument: 'Incarnation . . . becomes a matter of degree: God is incarnate in all men in so far as they are Spirit-filled, or Christ-like, or truly saintly'.[6] Years later Hick added the obvious conclusion: 'Incarnation in this sense has occurred and is occurring in many different ways and degrees in many different persons.'[7] Hick seems to expect that the divine spirit will act in essentially the same sort of way everywhere. Hence, the degree of human responsiveness will determine the degree of incarnation that we might recognize in different individuals. Such a reduction of 'incarnation' to the degrees of embodiment of unselfish love and of openness to the divine spirit rules out, however, the chance of doing anything more than calling Jesus a special, maybe even the highest available, example of such 'incarnation', meaning (B). Since such incarnation is only a matter of degree, Jesus can only be a special but not a unique case. Unique cases are in principle the only ones of their kind.[8]

Beyond Christianity

Before and beyond Christianity, one can find many examples of those who believed that, for a limited time or on a permanent basis, souls or other spiritual beings are embodied (or re-embodied, that is to say, reincarnated) in physical forms, human or otherwise. Thus Plato and his followers wrote of pre-existent souls being 'incarnated' for a time in human bodies. At Lystra in Asia Minor, when St Paul cured someone crippled from birth, an enthusiastic crowd imagined that they were experiencing a temporary manifestation of some deities that had descended from heaven. They shouted out 'the gods have come among us' and gave Paul the name of Hermes, and Paul's companion, Barnabas, the name of Zeus (Acts 14.8–13).

Platonic and similar notions about the 'embodying' of spirits differ from the classic or (A) meaning of incarnation on at least four grounds. First, it is not an embodiment that is freely chosen. Often enough, as in Indian views of reincarnation, the new embodiment follows automatically from the merits or demerits of a previous existence. Second, the soul or spirit that is embodied in a human form is not a complete person, still less a divine person. Third, the soul or spirit in question may be embodied in an animal or some other reality 'lower' down on the scale from human beings; or else, after having once been embodied in a human form, the soul or spirit may now be reincarnated into a non-human form. Fourth, such an 'incarnation' or 'reincarnation' is not normally claimed to take place for the good of others, let alone alleged to involve the project of saving the world, as in the case of the (A) meaning of incarnation.

We also note how a Platonic-style embodying of spirits also diverges from meaning (B) above. First, it is a question of a spirit or soul that is embodied in a visible form, and not simply qualities or attributes like charm and openness to God: as in 'she was the very incarnation of charm'; and 'he was the incarnation of openness to God'. Second, the agent who embodies some quality or attribute, whether a good or evil one, does so freely, whereas the pre-existent soul being incarnated for the first time (or returning for a second or further time, as in reincarnation) does so inevitably and has no choice in the matter. In the case of reincarnation such souls suffer and/or are punished as a necessary consequence for their past misdeeds. Third, the case of a Voldemort or an 'incarnation of supreme evil' introduces an element, sheer evil, which an extended use of 'incarnation' language, meaning (B), allows for, but which is normally absent from talk of embodied souls and spirits. This difference holds true even more of the Srivaishnava doctrine of *Avatara*, to which I now turn.

The fourth chapter of the *Bhagavadgita*, which for many Christians is the most accessible and attractive sacred book of Hinduism, provides a dialogue between the Lord Krishna, an avatar of Vishnu, and his disciple, the prince Arjuna. The passage suggests that one might compare such an *avatar* with the incarnation in its primary or (A) meaning. Of his own free will the Lord comes to earth to destroy evil and restore the declining life of the Vedic religion. His coming enables the virtuous people who worship him 'to behold him as he is, to see his deeds and listen to his words'.[9] But, despite such similarities between the incarnation in meaning (A) and *avatars,* commentators draw attention to major differences. First, orthodox Christianity accepts only one incarnation of the Word of God. Vaishnava Hinduism proposes ten or more primary or 'full' *avatars* or descents of God to earth, as well as many secondary and partial ones. Thus Vishnu is credited with ten primary *avatars.*[10] Second, unlike the Christian belief in one *human* incarnation, several of Vishnu's *avatars* occur as descents into such non-human forms as those of a fish, a tortoise or a bear. Third, when Vishnu descends and for a time takes on various bodily forms or manifestations, as a god, a human being or some other kind of being, his body is only apparently a material one; it is not made of ordinary matter. For Christians, however, the incarnate Son of God took on a true material body and not one that was only outwardly identical with ordinary human bodies. Fourth, the Hindu *avatars* use superhuman powers to defeat evil figures, rescue good people and restore a righteous order. Then they either die (but not a death understood as self-sacrifice) or return miraculously to the heavenly world. The conflict with evil powers for the incarnate Son of God, however, led to his sacrificial death, which took the horrendous form of crucifixion and was followed by a glorious resurrection. The resurrection of the crucified One (with the outpouring of the Holy Spirit) – a belief not to be found in Hindu thought – was the final outcome of the Son of God's incarnation. It broke the power of sin and death, and promised to repentant sinners a share in Christ's final victory both here and now and in the eternal life to come.

Before leaving Hinduism let me note an intriguing similarity between a revisionist version of *avatars* and Hick's Christian, revisionist version of the incarnation. Carman points out what has often happened to the Hindu belief about

the supreme Lord of the universe descending in human form
to spend time in the company of earthly creatures. 'Many
Hindus', Carman writes, 'treat their own gurus as avatars,
and the modern Hindu philosopher Radhakrishnan consid-
ers any perfected human being to be an avatar.'[11] Such Hindu
'avatars' look rather like Hick's occurrences of 'incarnation' in
numerous Spirit-filled persons.

This opening chapter has been a mapping exercise. It has
attempted to clarify the primary meaning of 'incarnation' for
mainline Christian faith. What will now concern us is the
primary meaning of what seems peculiar to Christianity, the
belief in one incarnation of the Son of God who with self-
giving love took on a fully human existence to live, die and
rise for the full and final welfare of all human beings and
their world.

Notes

1. See D. P. Jamros, 'Hegel on the Incarnation', *Theological Studies*
   56 (1995), 276–300.
2. D. F. Strauss, *The Life of Jesus Critically Examined*, trans. George
   Eliot (London: SCM Press, 1973), 779–80.
3. J. Campbell, *The Hero with a Thousand Faces* (London: Sphere
   Books, 1975), 37, 39, 272, 330.
4. J. Hick, *The Metaphor of God Incarnate* (London: SCM Press,
   1993), ix; see *ibid.*, 12, 105, 106, 152.
5. *Ibid.*, 163.
6. *Theology* 80 (1977), 205.
7. *The Metaphor of God Incarnate*, 111.
8. On Hick, see further G. O'Collins, 'The Incarnation Under Fire', in
   G. O'Collins and D. Kendall, *Focus on Jesus* (Leominster:
   Gracewing, 1996), 30–46.
9. J. B. Carman, 'Avatar and Incarnation', in *Majesty and Meekness*
   (Grand Rapids, Michigan: Eerdmans, 1994), 188–212, at 192.
10. For a list of the ten primary *avatars*, see *ibid.*, 210–12.
11. *Ibid.*, 191.

2

The Antecedents of the Incarnation

In the beginning was the Word and the Word was with God and the Word was God . . . And the Word was made flesh and made his home among us. (John 1.1, 14)

There is an infinite difference between the power and knowledge of the pre-incarnate Word and the powerlessness and ignorance of Jesus at birth. So how could there be continuity? But even supposing continuity, we might wonder whether the enormous difference between the two states is compatible with personal identity. (Peter Forrest, 'The Incarnation: A Philosophical Case for Kenosis', *Religious Studies* 36, 2000)

The personal pre-existence of the Word or Son of God is a necessary presupposition for any orthodox belief in the incarnation or the Word 'becoming flesh'. The incarnation means that a new person did not come on the scene when Jesus of Nazareth was conceived and born. And yet how is it possible for the human being Jesus to be the same person as or numerically identical with the pre-incarnate Word? Can and should we replace a 'strong', personal view of pre-existence with a 'soft' view which holds that Jesus, while not yet personally there, 'pre-existed' in evolving creation, in the history of humanity, and in the history of the Jewish people?

What should be said about views which, so far from reducing or minimalizing pre-existence, go beyond personal pre-existence to hold that the individual humanity of Jesus in some real sense was there before his conception? If we agree in rejecting both the minimalizing and maximalizing interpretations, we are still left with other questions. To what extent, if any, did earlier Jewish beliefs prepare the ground and supply the language for the startling Christian claim about the incarnation of a pre-existing divine person? And when did Christians first start expressing, more or less clearly, such a claim? And why might such a claim still matter for Christian faith and life?

Personal pre-existence

Orthodox Christian faith believes that Jesus of Nazareth was and is personally identical with the eternally pre-existent Son of God. Here, Christians maintain the pre-existence of a divine person, something distinct from a Jewish view of the pre-existence of the divine law (Torah) which was eventually communicated through Moses, or from Plato's scheme of pre-existing ideas which provided patterns for the demiurge in fashioning the world.

Such belief in pre-existence holds that Christ's personal existence is that of an eternal Subject within the oneness of God, and hence cannot be derived from the history of human beings and their world. Christ's personal being did not originate when his visible human history began. He did not come into existence as a new person around 5 BC, the date normally accepted for his birth. He exists personally as the eternal Son or Word of God. One can adopt here tensed language from the First Council of Nicea (AD 325) and state that 'there never was [a time] when he was not' (DH 126; ND 8) or that Christ 'always existed'. This language could, however, be misleading. Through sharing in the divine attribute of eternity, he exists timelessly, given that eternity itself is timeless. Eternity and eternal life, I would argue, are not to be reduced to temporal duration. The eternal 'now' of the divine existence means perfect union and simplicity in unchangeable fullness of life, with no parts and no relations of before and after, no having-been and no going-to-be.[1]

These reflections also suggest some dangers in the very term 'pre-existence'. To speak of Christ pre-existing his incarnation and the very creation of the world (when time began) could be wrongly taken to imply a 'before' and 'after' for his personal, divine existence. An addition that the First Council of Constantinople (AD 381) made to the Nicene Creed, 'begotten from the Father *before all ages*' (DH 150; ND 12) might mislead us into thinking of a temporal succession as if the Son merely preceded or antedated everything that later began in and with time. Pre-existence means, rather, that Christ personally belongs to an order of being other than the created, temporal one. His personal, divine existence transcends or goes beyond temporal (and spatial) categories; it might be better expressed as trans-existence, meta-existence, or, quite simply, eternal existence.

None of this is intended to allege that eternity and time have nothing to do with each other or are utterly alien to each other, even to the point of being mutually exclusive in a total way. If that were so, the eternal God could not have produced a world of time. Eternity transcends time but without being apart from it; eternity and time should be considered together. Through the attribute of eternity, God is present immediately and powerfully to all times. In the incarnation this presence went so far that the eternally existing Son of God took on temporality or a human existence in time.

A soft view of pre-existence

Difficulties over personal pre-existence lead some authors to revise this belief in such a fashion as to explain it away. Thus, John Macquarrie argues that Jesus pre-existed only in the sense of his (1) being elected for his role and pre-ordained from the beginning in the mind or purpose of God (= an intentional pre-existence), as well as Jesus' (2) being previously 'there' in the evolving cosmos, the history of the human race, and the particular history of Israel.

Macquarrie assures his readers that (1) is 'a very high degree of reality'. Yet it is almost indistinguishable from any human being's form of pre-existence in the eternal purposes of God.[2] Macquarrie's explanation recalls the 'choosing' and 'predestining' of all of us 'before the foundation of the world' – a message with which the Letter to the Ephesians opens (1.4–5). The other point made in Macquarrie's account of pre-existence (2) is an illusion if he thinks that it says anything special which would set Christ apart. We could say of any human person whatsoever that he or she had been 'there' in the evolving cosmos, in the history of the whole human race, and in the particular history of his or her people and culture. The pre-existent 'Son of God' of John's prologue, Philippians 2.6–8, and the opening chapter of Hebrews, is not to be reduced to mere divine intention or what we might call an 'intentional' existence. The Son of God personally pre-existed everything that was created and all human history. He was not a simple possibility or idea which eventually became actualized as a person with an incarnation in 5 BC. Besides being incompatible with NT and post-NT Christian faith, such an explanation would be trivial, because it is true of all of us.

Maximalizing excesses

In minimalizing the meaning of personal pre-existence, Macquarrie may have been reacting to some who maintain or at least hint at some kind of real pre-existence for Jesus' humanity. In the third century Origen held that Christ's human soul pre-existed the incarnation, a view subsequently rejected by official teaching (DH 404–05; ND 618/2,3). Without going as far as that, some modern writers have suggested or at least hinted at a continuity in human consciousness and memory between the earthly Jesus and the pre-incarnate Son of God. Some are not content with arguing (correctly) that the earthly Jesus was humanly aware of this divine identity. They raise and answer affirmatively a further question. Through his human consciousness was Jesus also aware of his eternal, personal pre-existence as Son of God? Could he, through his human powers, recollect a heavenly past and enjoy memories of his pre-incarnate state?

Thus in a 1981 document, 'Theology, Christology and Anthropology', the International Theological Commission claimed that 'at least in an indirect fashion', Jesus showed that he was conscious of 'his eternal existence as Son of the Father'. The second proposition of the Commission's 1985 document, 'The Consciousness of Christ concerning Himself and his Mission', went even further in maintaining the following questionable claim: 'The consciousness Jesus has of his mission also involves . . . the consciousness of his "pre-existence". The mission (in time), in fact, is not essentially separable from his (eternal) procession; it is its prolongation'. Hence Jesus' 'human consciousness of his own mission "translates", so to speak, the eternal relationship with the Father into the idiom of a human life'.[3]

Let me explain more clearly what is at issue here. Many NT scholars hold that in his words and works the earthly Jesus claimed a truly divine authority and showed that he was aware of standing in a unique relationship to the God whom he called 'Abba' or 'Father dear'. Jesus lived out his ministry conscious of being *the* Son. But was he also conscious – at least implicitly and in an indirect fashion – of existing eternally before his human conception and birth? Obviously much depends here on how one understands 'implicitly' and 'indirectly' and how an implicit and indirect consciousness might possibly work. But I fear that at least in some sense of these words the International Theological Commission detected in Christ's human consciousness an awareness of his eternal pre-existence. Such a position comes very close to alleging that through his human memory he at least half-remembered such a pre-existence. This would be to ignore the fact that his human memory, along with his human consciousness and all his other human powers, began to exist only when he was conceived and born.

With the incarnation the Son of God becomes fully human *and newly human*. 'Before' the incarnation he was a human being only in God's intention and 'not yet' a human being in fact. It may be that some of those who puzzle over Jesus being personally identical with the eternal Son of God imagine that this mysterious personal continuity may be based on some kind of continuity in his human mind and/or memory.

Those who more or less identify persons with minds must feel the pressure here to postulate some continuity of (human) mind between the pre-existent Son of God and the earthly Jesus. Same person, same mind, they argue. Something similar holds true of those for whom memory defines, or at least helps to define, the self. For them memory will constitute the identity-in-continuity of Jesus' self and so his being identical with the Son of God. Hence Jesus, when he grows up, will have not only memories of the earthly life which is already behind him but also some sort of memories of what is much further 'behind' him, his pre-incarnational heavenly life.[4]

To take these routes in accounting for the personal continuity between the eternal Son of God and the earthly Jesus underestimates two facts. First, the humanity of Jesus, which includes his mind and memory, came into existence only with his conception and birth. There was no pre-existent humanity; his human mind and memory were not there 'before'. Second, the human mind and memory have a physical aspect to them. Although not reducible to and fully explained by the brain and its functions, mind and memory do not work alone and in isolation from the brain. Those who imagine Jesus' consciousness and memory functioning 'before' incarnation – for example, in storing up pre-incarnational memories – would have to postulate the pre-existence of something like a physical brain. How otherwise would they account for mind and memory operating in that pre-incarnation state? Or do they want to endorse again Origen's theory of Jesus' pre-existent soul with its thoughts, decisions and memories?

Antecedent beliefs

The first Christians fashioned their proclamation and interpretation of Jesus largely by putting together two elements: on the one hand, their experience of events in which Jesus was the central protagonist, and, on the other hand, the ready-made images and concepts they found to be illuminating and relevant in their inherited Jewish faith and Scriptures. To articulate their convictions about Jesus and his role in fulfilling the divine purposes, they drew on the ideas, beliefs and expectations of Judaism. They depended above all on the OT Scriptures, which they quarried for expressions to express their experience of and faith in Jesus. What language and concepts were significant when they spoke and wrote about Jesus' personal pre-existence? The OT themes of 'word', 'wisdom' and 'the angel of the Lord' proved particularly relevant.

The Psalms celebrate the creative and conserving Word of God, which 'created the heavens' (Psalms 33.6). The 'Word' also expresses God's revelation mediated through the OT prophets. The Word of the Lord comes to them; hence they can communicate divine oracles and declare, 'Thus says the Lord.' 'Word' also personifies the divine activity in the story of the chosen people's deliverance from Egypt, at least when death comes to the firstborn of the Egyptians (Wisdom 18.15–16).

As a personification of God's creative, revealing and saving activity, 'Wisdom' functions even more strikingly. Begotten 'long ago' as God's firstborn, Lady Wisdom not only exists with God before everything else but also co-operates in the divine work of creation (Proverbs 8.30–1). She is depicted as building her house and inviting the simple to join her feast of food and wine, which symbolize the doctrine and virtue that come from God (Proverbs 9.1–6). She follows the divine choice of Israel and makes her home in Jerusalem. Once settled in the holy city, Lady Wisdom sends out an invitation to her great banquet: 'Come to me, you who desire me, and eat your fill of my fruits. For the memory of me is sweeter than honey, and the possession of me sweeter than the honeycomb' (Sirach 24.19–20). Here Wisdom is food and drink, the divine source of nourishment and life. A very late book of the OT portrays Wisdom as all-powerful, penetrating and pervading all things (Wisdom 7.22–4); 'she reaches mightily from one end of the earth to the other, and she orders all things well' (Wisdom 8.1). She can even be called 'a reflection of eternal light' or 'a spotless mirror of the working of God' (Wisdom 7.26). The theme of unity between Wisdom and God reaches a climax when the biblical author reinterprets Israel's history and attributes to Wisdom the saving deeds normally attributed to God. Through Moses she delivered the Hebrew people in the Exodus (Wisdom 10.15–18). Even more than Word, Wisdom functions as a vivid personification of the creative, revealing and saving activity of God. But, as we shall see in a moment, it is a giant leap from the language of personification to recognize in Jesus a distinct person, the pre-existent divine Word and Wisdom who is now incarnated.

Accounts of theophanies or appearances of God in the OT, especially those involving talk of an 'Angel of the Lord' or a kind of otherworldly double for God, also contributed to the way Christians could imagine and speak of the visible coming among them of a pre-existent divine person. An 'Angel' or messenger of the Lord could act and speak with the authority of God; at times the Angel's appearing can hardly be distinguished from that of God. Thus 'the Angel of the Lord', who appears to Moses in a flame of fire out of a bush, becomes the Lord God who reveals the divine name of 'I am who I am' and sends Moses to liberate a suffering people (Exodus 3.1–15). In these and similar texts (e.g. the appearance to Hagar in Genesis 16.7–14 and the instructions to Abraham in Genesis 22.1–19) the angelic figure personally represents God and even speaks as God. This way of presenting theophanies also helped to prepare the ground and the language for the Christian belief in the incarnation of a distinct, pre-existent divine person.

Nevertheless, this Christian belief was a startling novelty. Geza Vermes makes this point forcefully: 'in the minds of first-century Palestinian Jews no human being . . . could conceivably share the nature of the Almighty'.[5] Certainly it was very un-Jewish to recognize in a human being a pre-existent divine being come among us. How could such a faith be reconciled with genuine monotheism, or belief in one (and only one) personal God? But the new Christian faith, while not abandoning monotheism, did acknowledge what a later age could call a personal distinction within God that would allow for the incarnation. To express their new faith, Christians drew on the language and figures they had inherited, and in a special way on the themes of Word, Wisdom and the Angel of the Lord.

Paul and pre-existence

The letters of the first Christian writer, St Paul, characteristically depict Jesus as divine Lord and Son of God, whose identity and redemptive work have been revealed by his resurrection from the dead and exaltation to the Father's right hand. For various reasons, not least his Damascus road encounter with the living Son of God (1 Corinthians 15.8; Galatians 1.11–17), Paul proclaimed constantly the 'post-existent' Christ: that is to say, the divine Lord who exists after his death, resurrection and exaltation. Nevertheless, even if the apostle does not elaborate them at length, we find in his letters a number of precious references to the pre-existent Son of God.

Paul writes of the divine, pre-existent One not only as being 'sent' by the Father (Romans 8.3; Galatians 4.4) but also as taking the initiative by 'becoming poor' for our sake (2 Corinthians 8.9) in 'emptying himself, taking the form of a slave', and being 'born in human likeness' (Philippians 2.7). The apostle's language suggests concisely the impoverishment and self-limitation entailed by the incarnation; we return to this later.

To be sure, Paul does not focus on the Son of God's pre-existence; he is much more interested in what the Son of God came or was sent to do – namely, to free human beings from the forces of evil, enable them to become God's adopted sons and daughters, and let them live with the power of the indwelling Spirit (e.g. Galatians 4.4–7). Despite this predominant focus on Christ's post-existence, Paul offers some striking passages that involve pre-existence, not least his new version of the 'Shema'.

The central Jewish prayer, called the 'Shema' from its first word in Hebrew ('Listen!') came from Deuteronomy 6.4–9; 11.13–21 (see also Numbers 15.37–41) and classically expressed the Jewish faith in one God. In 1 Corinthians 8.6,

Paul takes up this very familiar confession and inserts the Son of God into its heart; what he wants to say is that 'for us Christians' our faith in the one God now includes Jesus Christ. A striking feature of this passage is that the apostle does not pause to argue for this new form of monotheistic faith; he takes it for granted that his readers in Corinth will agree with him. The passage runs as follows: 'For us there is *one* God, the Father, from whom are all things and for whom we exist, and *one* Lord Jesus Christ, through whom are all things and through whom we exist.' Paul has taken from the Shema 'God', to be identified now with 'the Father', and 'Lord' to be identified now with 'Jesus Christ', understood to be 'the Son'. The apostle not only introduces these 'glosses' but also twice adds a reference to the divine work of creation. The Son, in particular, is identified as the One 'through whom are all things and through whom we exist'. Paul describes the Son as active in creation, and hence pre-existent and 'there' in the divine life to be able to play that role. A later letter by Paul or one of his disciples will spell out more fully the creative work of the Son (Colossians 1.16–17). But already in 1 Corinthians the apostle (and with him the Christians of Corinth) acknowledge the *person* of Jesus Christ to have pre-existed and collaborated in the work of creation, a role the OT Scriptures had attributed to those *personifications* of divine activity, Word and Wisdom.

Is pre-existence important?

Belief in the pre-existent Son who comes or is sent into the world does not lack spiritual and theological cash value. This belief strongly underlines the divine love for human beings and their world. To have continued sending prophets would cost God nothing, so to speak. But the coming and personal presence of the pre-existent Son of God uniquely expresses the divine desire to be with us, to share our sufferings and redeem us from our desperate situation. Anything less than this might well leave us wondering how much we matter to God. 'God so loved the world that he gave his only Son' (John 3.16) is convincing in a way that a 'lesser' text would not be: for instance, 'God so loved the world that he sent another great prophet.' As a traditional Christmas message put it, 'God cared enough to send the best.' Seen this way, the doctrine of personal pre-existence contributes vitally to the full power of the incarnation message.

Belief in the personal pre-existence of the Word of God holds together beautifully the doctrines of creation and redemption. The central protagonist of the drama of redemption was/is already active in creating and conserving the universe. The Creator and the Redeemer are personally identical. As much as anyone, St Irenaeus of Lyons (d. *c.* 200) saw the importance of this. In every part of the world and for all members of the human race, thanks to his creative role, the Son is always present and active: 'from the beginning, the Son, being present in his creation, reveals his Father' (*Adversus Haereses*, 4.20.6–7); and – we would add – this revelation is salvific and aimed at bringing everyone home to the life-giving glory of God.

Christian tradition and liturgy have endorsed and delighted in the personal pre-existence of the Son. The Nicene-Constantinopolitan Creed, which came from the First Council of Nicea (AD 325) and the First Council of Constantinople (AD 381), is the most significant confession of Christian faith, one shared by all Christians, both Eastern and Western. It confesses the eternal, personal existence of the Son of God before moving to his becoming incarnate through the Holy Spirit and the Virgin Mary. A lovely liturgical tribute to the pre-existence of Christ comes on 18 December, on the second day of the immediate preparation for the celebration of the Christmas. The antiphon at Evening Prayer endorses faith in the pre-existent One who actively engaged in the history of Israel and was personally present as Lord ('Adonai') and Leader long before his incarnation into our world: 'O Adonai and Leader of Israel, you appeared to Moses in a burning bush and you gave him the Law on Sinai. O come and save us with your mighty power.'

Notes

1. For further lines of thought see W. L. Craig, 'Eternity', in A. Hastings *et al.* (eds), *The Oxford Companion to Christian Thought* (Oxford: Oxford University Press, 2000), 210–12; G. Loughlin, 'Time', *ibid.*, 707–9.
2. J. Macquarrie, *Jesus Christ in Modern Thought* (London: SCM Press, 1990), 121, 390–2; see N. Coll, *Christ in Eternity and Time. Modern Anglican Perspectives* (Dublin: Four Courts, 2001).
3. For these texts of the International Theological Commission, see M. Sharkey (ed.), *International Theological Commission: Texts and Documents 1969–1985* (San Francisco: Ignatius Press, 1989), 207–23, at 217; 305–16, at 310.
4. On personal continuity see C. S. Evans, 'The Self-Emptying of Love: Some Thoughts on Kenotic Christology', in S. Davis, D. Kendall and G. O'Collins (eds), *The Incarnation* (Oxford: Oxford University Press, 2002), 246–72, at 267–72.
5. G. Vermes, *The Changing Faces of Jesus* (London: Penguin Press, 2000), 207.

3

The Incarnation and its Aftermath

Bethlehem and Golgotha cannot be separated. The incarnation of the Son of God created the premises and the foundation for that mighty, earth-shaking event when the Son of God died on Golgotha for our salvation. It is this death for our salvation that gives the incarnation its ultimate, terrible solemnity. (Karl Adam, *The Christ of Faith*)

'God has been born', they [the Magi] cried, 'we have seen him ourselves. The World is saved. Nothing else matters.' (W. H. Auden, *For the Time Being: A Christmas Oratorio*)

With the primary meaning and the antecedents of the incarnation now clarified, at least provisionally, we turn to reflect on the full context of faith in the incarnation. To begin with, one must say this: to take a static view of the incarnation would be to isolate Christmas from Easter. The coming among us of the Word of God should be viewed dynamically and seen as closely intertwined not only with its antecedents (Chapter 2) but also, and even more, with what was to follow.

The first Christians

Among the NT writers themselves, Paul, as we saw in the last chapter, has something to say about the pre-existent life of the incarnate Son of God but he also repeatedly connects the Son's coming with its aftermath: the death and resurrection of Jesus, the outpouring of the Holy Spirit (e.g. Galatians 4.4–7), and the final coming of the glorious Lord (e.g. 1 Corinthians 11.26). Admittedly, however, apart from witnessing to Jesus' Jewish background and his celebration of the Last Supper, the apostle has little to report from the story of the Incarnate One. He quotes a few sayings, but has nothing to say about the baptism of Jesus, the preaching of the kingdom and Jesus' miracles that visibly symbolized the presence of God's reign and rule.

In this sense John's Gospel presents a more complete picture of the incarnation and its aftermath. After announcing that 'the Word became flesh and made his home among us', John includes a number of miracles and much teaching from the Incarnate One. Furthermore, even in his opening chapter John reaches forward to the final drama of Christ's earthly existence by announcing him as 'the Lamb of God who takes away the sin of the world' (John 1.29; see 1.36). This theme will turn up at the end when Jesus was crucified at the hour when the paschal lambs were killed in the Temple precincts; to drive home the parallelism, the evangelist records that Jesus' legs were not broken on the cross and then introduces the rule against breaking the bones of the paschal lambs (John 19.36). Paul and John, when read together, set a wonderful standard by presenting the incarnation in a fuller, dynamic setting, which includes the ministry, crucifixion and resurrection.

Paul and John, two towering thinkers from the NT church, do not stand alone in appreciating the proper, wider setting for confessing the incarnation. Matthew and Luke, for instance, recognize in their own way the wider setting of the incarnation. Matthew's account of Jesus' conception and birth reaches not only back to Abraham and Sarah (Matthew 1.1–17) but also forward – not least through the story of the Magi and the massacre of the Holy Innocents (Matthew 2.1–18), which anticipate the savagery of Jesus' crucifixion and the glory of his resurrection. Readers of Matthew notice easily enough the connection between the newly conceived Jesus named as Emmanuel or 'God with us' (Matthew 1.23) and the promise that comes at the very end from the crucified and risen Jesus: 'I will be with you all days, even to the end of time' (Matthew 28.20). Lines are drawn between the incarnation of the Son of God and the close of all history; the beginning and the end are linked. But what readers can miss is the careful way in which the opening story of the wise men and the escape of the Holy Family match the final events where two women disciples are involved at the death, burial and resurrection of Jesus. Matthew's account of Jesus' birth sets the wise men and the Holy Family over against the power and trickery of King Herod, who plots to do away with the Christ Child. But because of a dream and the action of 'an angel of the Lord' (Matthew 2.12–13), Mary and Joseph saved the Christ Child by fleeing into Egypt, and the Magi take another route home and so avoid Herod. God's friends, the Holy Family and the wise men, seem few and weak. But through special divine action they all escape the crafty scheming of a ruthless king. At the end of Matthew's Gospel, once again 'an angel of the Lord' (Matthew 28.3–7) will come on the scene, not only to make the resurrection known but also to terrify the guard, those representatives of worldly might who conspire against Jesus and his followers. Matthew (from 27.61) repeatedly contrasts Mary Magdalene and another Mary with the squad of soldiers. Two unarmed women, instructed by God's angel, become the first human beings to hear and announce the uniquely good news of the

resurrection. They will be the first to see the risen Jesus
(Matthew 28.8–10). The power with which the glorious angel
speaks and acts turns the tables effortlessly on the rulers of
this world who have put Jesus to death. In changing the
course of events, God takes good care of his own Son and
those who love him. Matthew's beautifully told story draws
clear lines from the incarnation to the resurrection of the crucified Jesus and beyond.

Luke's Gospel also uses a genealogy to associate the incarnation and the birth of Jesus with what has gone before – in
this case by tracing Jesus' ancestry back to Adam, God's first
'son' (Luke 3.23–38). Most readers readily spot the connection Luke makes between Christ's birth and his coming death
when old Simeon warns Mary: 'This child is destined for the
falling and rising of many in Israel, and to be a sign that will
be opposed . . . and a sword will pierce your own soul too' (Luke
2.34–5). But there is much more to the ties Luke establishes
between Christ's birth and its aftermath. Take, for example,
the Holy Spirit. The Spirit's activity at the conception of Jesus
(Luke 1.33–5) opens a whole process of Christ being enfleshed
in history, a process which includes the baptism when the
Spirit anoints him for his priestly, prophetic and kingly
ministry (Luke 3.22; Acts 10.38), the opening message of
Jesus (Luke 4.17–21), his mighty deeds worked with the
power of the Spirit, and the sending of the Spirit who has been
promised by the Father (Luke 24.49; Acts 2.33). Rather than
leaving the incarnation as an isolated event, Luke shows how
it initiates a dramatic story in which Jesus is revealed to be
the bearer and giver of the Spirit. Like Paul, John, and other
NT authors, Luke and Matthew never set the incarnation
apart from its antecedents and its aftermath.

But what of the post-NT tradition and liturgical life of the
Church? Does it and how does it link the incarnation with
what went before and, even more, with what followed the
Word becoming flesh?

The law of praying

Here, if anywhere, 'the law of praying' should shape both 'the law of believing' and the theological reflection that follows from and articulates faith. A liturgical prayer shared by all Christians, the Nicene-Constantinopolitan Creed of 381, points the way to a dynamic view of the incarnation, taken in the context of its antecedents and its aftermath. The Creed recalls the eternal life of the Son of God and his role in creation ('through him all things were made') before confessing: 'For us and for our salvation he came down from heaven: by the power of the Holy Spirit he became incarnate from the Virgin Mary and was made man.' But the credally expressed faith does not stop there. It presses on to confess Christ's crucifixion, his resurrection, his ascension into heaven, and future coming in glory at the end of history. This Creed, used by Eastern Christians at baptism and by Western Christians at the Eucharist, shows splendidly what it is to put the incarnation in the dynamic context of an extended story.

What we find in the Nicene-Constantinopolitan Creed we find also in the Apostles' Creed. The confession of the incarnation, 'he was conceived by the power of the Holy Spirit and born of the Virgin Mary', is preceded by a brief reference to the Son's 'prior', eternal life with God the Father and followed by what comes after the incarnation – in Christ's death, descent to the dead,[1] resurrection, ascension and future coming to judge the living and the dead. Thus the other major creed of Western Christianity, the Apostles' Creed, also witnesses to the need to appreciate the whole, dramatic meaning of the incarnation in the context of what precedes it and of all that follows from it.

The *Apostolic Tradition*, which was composed by St Hippolytus in the early third century and which provided Roman Catholics with the basic text for their second eucharistic prayer of 1970, put the incarnation in a setting which ran from the Son's eternal pre-existence to the resurrection. Let me quote the relevant part, taking it from Gregory Dix's translation and using his numeration:

> 4 We render thanks unto thee, O God, through Thy Beloved Child Jesus Christ, Whom in these last times Thou didst send to us [to be] a Saviour and Redeemer and the Angel of Thy counsel;
> 5 Who is Thy Word inseparable [from Thee], through Whom Thou madest all things and in Whom Thou wast well pleased;
> 6 [Whom] Thou didst send from heaven into [the] Virgin's womb and Who conceived within her was made flesh and demonstrated to be Thy Son being born of Holy Spirit and a Virgin;
> 7 Who fulfilling Thy will and preparing for Thee a holy people stretched forth His hands for suffering that He might release from sufferings them who have believed in Thee;
> 8 Who when He was betrayed to voluntary suffering that He might abolish death and rend the bonds of the devil and tread down hell and enlighten the righteous and . . . demonstrate the resurrection . . .[2]

Here the incarnation (6) is preceded by the Son's eternal existence with the Father and role in creation (4–5), and followed by the incarnate Son's passion and resurrection (7–8).

This full context of *The Apostolic Tradition* is lacking when, in an otherwise moving passage, Karl Adam links Bethlehem and Golgotha but leaves it at that:

> The incarnation of the Son of God created the premises and foundation for that mighty, earth-shaking event when the Son of God died on Golgotha for our salvation. It is this death for our salvation that gives the incarna-

tion its ultimate, terrible solemnity, and its special importance: the Son of God was born for us, that he might die for us.[3]

Let us see how significant voices from the Christian tradition handled the complete, narrative setting of the incarnation. Do they witness for the case of interpreting the incarnation dynamically and against those who would pluck it out of its full context?

Voices from the past

In his major work *De Incarnatione* ('On the Incarnation') St Athanasius of Alexandria (d. 373) expounded and defended the incarnation in the light of what it led to: the teaching and miracles of Christ and their aftermath in the sacrifice of the crucifixion (nos. 20–5) and the resurrection (nos. 26–32). Through his union with humanity, the Word of God restored to sinful men and women the divine image in which they had been created. By dying and rising he overcame death, the result of sin. Thus Athanasius succeeded in relating the incarnation to the whole story of the incarnate Son of God.

Through a series of brilliant antitheses a Christmas sermon by St Augustine of Hippo (354–430) highlighted what the Son of God, 'he who was before all ages', underwent after being 'made in the mother whom he himself made'. 'The Ruler of the stars' came to experience hunger, thirst, weariness and, finally, torture and death. Divine 'Strength' was made weak and the One who was 'Life' itself died. All of this took place to set free 'the undeserving' and share with them 'such great and good things' (*Sermon* 191). Far from preaching in isolation of the Son of God's being 'made' in a mother at his incarnation, Augustine looked back to the Son's existence 'before all ages' and forward to the death on a cross which would bring salvation to 'the undeserving'. Thus

Augustine framed the event of the incarnation in its full
setting.

Many recall that St Thomas Aquinas (d. 1274) initiated
his christological reflections with the incarnation, but do not
always note that Aquinas went on further. In the third part of
his *Summa theologiae*, he moved forward from the incarnation to examine the life, death and resurrection of Christ, as
well as his continuing presence through the Eucharist and
the other sacraments.

Martin Luther (1483–1546), in *The Small Catechism* and
The Large Catechism (both produced in 1529), took the
Apostles' Creed as his catechetical grid. That meant expounding the incarnation within the whole history of salvation – in
the context of its antecedents and aftermath.

Luther's contemporary, St Ignatius of Loyola (1491–1556),
makes the incarnation the first contemplation in the 'second
week' of his 30-day *Spiritual Exercises*. He imagines the
three persons of the Trinity 'decreeing' from all eternity that
the second person would assume human nature to save all
men and women (nos. 101–2). Then follows a contemplation
of the nativity, the event in which 'the great Lord of all things
began his life on earth in lowliest poverty' – a life in which for
our sake he was to be 'hungry, thirsty, sweating, shivering,
insulted, beaten up', and, at the end, crucified (no. 116). The
second and third weeks of the *Spiritual Exercises* take the
retreatants through many episodes of Jesus' life, suffering
and death. Then the fourth or final week leads on to the story
of the resurrection. The contemplation on the incarnation is
pivotal, but, far from standing in splendid isolation, it is skil-
fully integrated into what prepared the way for Christ's
coming and, even more, into what followed that coming.

Poets and painters have continued to play their part in
handing on the great Christian tradition. Over and over
again they have treated the incarnation as a high point in one
long drama of divine action for human beings. In 'The

Journey of the Magi' T. S. Eliot (1888–1965) discreetly hints at the link between Bethlehem and Calvary, when in his old age one of the Magi recalls arriving at the time of Jesus' birth and wonders whether they had been led to witness a birth or a death. In *For the Time Being: A Christmas Oratorio*, W. H. Auden (1907–73) pictures Mary at the manger wondering: 'How soon will you start on the Sorrowful Way?' Auden sets the incarnation in its proper, fuller setting, not only by looking forward to Jesus' suffering which will begin with the flight into Egypt, but also by recalling creation and the story of Adam and Eve.

'Seeing Salvation', an exhibition held in the spring of 2000 at the National Gallery in London, began with the incarnation and birth of Jesus and took its viewers through to the resurrection of Christ and the general resurrection that the glorious Christ will bring. Right from the outset, through the works it included from Giovanni Bellini (d. 1516) and Bartolomé Murillo (1617–82) the exhibition signalled what was to come in the story of the newborn Jesus. In 'The Madonna of the Meadow' Bellini portrays the Christ Child sleeping across his Mother's lap in a posture obviously meant to prefigure what followed the deposition from the cross. In compositions of the 'Pietà' (Italian for pity or mercy) Christ will lie in Mary's lap, limp and lifeless in the sleep of death. To drive home the Christ Child's connection with his coming passion and death, Bellini adds at one side a sinister, dark bird perched on a bare tree – a clear pointer to the cross on which Jesus will die. Murillo's 'The Christ Child Resting on the Cross' much more blatantly anticipates what is to happen at the end of Jesus' public life. The Christ Child rests asleep and almost naked on a tiny cross, with a skull tucked under his arm.

The exhibition 'Seeing Salvation' brought together several major paintings that focus on the story of the Magi coming with their gifts of gold, frankincense and myrrh to worship

the Christ Child. The artists used the episode to associate
Jesus' birth with his coming death for all humanity. Christian tradition interpreted the gift of gold as homage to
Christ's kingship, the frankincense as homage to his divinity,
and the red grains of myrrh as alluding to his death and
embalming. Artists could exploit such items in the Magi story
to connect the incarnation and birth of Christ with their final
outcome in his death and resurrection that brought salvation
to all peoples.

Sometimes Western artists have linked the nativity with
the crucifixion by introducing cross-tipped pikes carried by
soldiers who accompany the Magi; or else they make the connection by picturing the Christ Child as loosely covered by a
shroud-like garment and shrinking back in fear from the
strange visitors. Some Eastern icons of the nativity turn the
manger into a tiny coffin made of stone, in which the Child
lies wrapped in grave-cloths.

One image that the exhibition 'Seeing Salvation' did not
include was that of Christ crucified on a lily. In medieval
England the scene of the Annunciation (Luke 1. 26–38) was
sometimes pictured with Mary and the angel standing on
either side of a lily on which Christ himself hangs. At that
time many believers thought that the date of the crucifixion
(in AD 33) coincided not only with that of the Annunciation to
Mary, 25 March, but also with the date of the creation of the
universe. Thus creation, incarnation and salvation were
believed to come together in a single divine outreach to the
world and all humanity.

The permanence of the incarnation

The humanity of Christ came into being with the incarnation. But will the humanity he assumed cease to be at the end
of human history? Or has it already ceased to be with the
resurrection? In rising from the dead, has the incarnate Son,

while remaining personally identical with the earthly Jesus, surrendered or left behind his humanity? Or should believers insist on the (now glorified) humanity remaining for ever? Some modern authors, such as Peter Forrest,[4] raise the question of the permanence of the incarnation. Forrest, albeit briefly and not very satisfactorily, answers the question in the affirmative. Why should we maintain that the incarnation is not a temporary state and will never be undone, so that the Incarnate One will remain human for ever?

This question differs from that raised at the beginning of the last chapter. There it was a matter of the *personal* continuity between the pre-existent Word of God (or Word of God existing 'before' creation and the incarnation) and Jesus of Nazareth. Here it is rather a question of a continuity between a pre-resurrection and a post-resurrection human nature, a continuity made possible by the fact that Christ's human existence, while wonderfully enhanced, does not disappear with the resurrection.

Mainstream Christians may well appeal here to three additions to the Nicene Creed of 325 made by the First Council of Constantinople in 381. This latter council confessed that the 'Lord Jesus Christ' now 'sits on the right hand of the Father', will come again 'with glory' to judge the living and the dead, and of his 'kingdom there will be no end'. The impact of the first two additions was to underline the divine identity of Jesus. He sits neither near nor under the divine throne but right alongside and on a par with the Father. His future coming in judgement will be accompanied with divine glory. Apropos of the permanence of Christ's post-Easter humanity a tough-minded adversary might argue: 'Both of these statements are quite true. But they refer to the divine Logos. The second person of the Trinity is on a par with the Father, and will show himself at the Last Judgement. But is anything here said clearly of the permanent (glorified) humanity?'

Let me delay for the moment any comment on the first two additions made by Constantinople I and look at the third addition: of his 'kingdom there will be no end'. In the historical context of the late fourth century the affirmation of Christ's endless kingdom, based on Luke 1.33, was directed against Marcellus of Ancyra (d. 374). He denied that the Word of God was a distinct *hypostasis* or person and argued that the divine Monad, after unfolding itself into a triad, would at the end reverse to an original unity as the divine Monad. Thus, as regards the second person of the Trinity, Marcellus limited the existence of the Son to a period of incarnation. Once the purposes of the incarnation have been achieved, the divine Monad will no longer manifest the relationship of sonship and will return to its original state. Hence, seven years after the death of Marcellus, the addition from Constantinople I about the Son's kingdom having no end bore more on the personal distinctions within God persisting for ever and not ending at some point. Here the Council wanted to confess something about the eternal life of the tripersonal God rather than precisely about the permanent status of the human condition assumed by the Son at a certain point in history.

The right way to argue here will lead us to reflect on the risen Christ not precisely *in himself* but *for us*. Let me explain. Those who take the first approach (through Christ in himself) will think about the permanence of the incarnation in terms of the risen Son of God maintaining in himself the union he had previously entered into with the human condition. In other words, he continues to have the same nature or individual humanity with which he had operated in his pre-risen state, even if that given nature has been dramatically transformed and glorified. This continuity, some argue, is to be established through a continuity of (human) mind and memories between the earthly and risen Son of God. In particular, the persistence of the same memories would point to the fact that his human nature, in which these memories are lodged, has not disappeared in his risen state. Such memories would show that, in his humanity, the risen Christ is continuous with the earthly Jesus. What makes this way of arguing extremely problematic, however, is our lack of access to any human mind and memories of the risen Christ. We have only a limited access to his mind and memories during his earthly existence. Where and how do we enjoy any access to that mind and memories beyond the resurrection?

Here it is worth observing that the Gospel narratives of the encounters with the risen Christ do not depict him as telling his disciples what it was like to recall previous personal experiences now that he is risen from the dead.[5] The Gospel of Mark ends with a promise of one or more meetings with the risen Christ (Mark 16.7) but does not include any account of such meetings. Two post-resurrection meetings occur at the end of Matthew's Gospel (Matthew 28.8–10, 16–20). The closest the narrative approaches attributing memories to the risen Jesus comes when he commands the eleven disciples to teach all nations 'to observe all that I have commanded you'. Here it is a question of the disciples carrying on Jesus' teaching ministry; the subject matter of their teaching has been indicated in the great discourses of Matthew's Gospel, especially the Sermon on the Mount. We would do violence to the text if we attempted to read it in terms of the risen Jesus himself remembering and recalling the content of his earthly teaching. The Easter chapter of Luke includes the theme of remembering, but it is a matter of Jesus' followers recalling things which they had heard him say (Luke 24.6–8, 44; see Acts 1.4). The two Easter chapters with which John's Gospel closes are full of haunting memories, but they are the memories for disciples (then) and for the readers (now) which are being evoked. The Fourth Evangelist never hints at memories going through the mind of the risen Jesus as if the risen One were recollecting in tranquillity his human history.

When the Gospel writers present a continuity between the
pre-Easter and the post-Easter Jesus, they do so not in terms
of some continuity *within* his own mind and memory, but
rather in terms of his revealing and redemptive activity *for
us*. The Jesus who built up his history by living as a human
being (that is to say, through the human nature he assumed)
is the same risen Jesus who meets his disciples and commis-
sions them for their mission, and, 'sitting on the right hand of
the Father', intercedes for them. His history, which, thanks to
his human nature, could be lived for others, rose with him in
a resurrection that initiated a new life for others. The eternal
significance of his history is essentially bound up with the
eternal significance of the humanity he assumed at the
incarnation.

The permanent existence and significance of Jesus'
humanity which are hinted at by the Gospels are more fully
spelled out by the Letters of Paul, the Book of Acts and the
Book of Revelation. What they have to say about the enduring
presence of the risen Jesus would be unthinkable if his
humanity had disappeared with his death and resurrection. In
fact, the proclamation of his resurrection would make no
sense, if the crucified Jesus had not been raised with a now
glorified humanity. In a concise formula Paul sums up what
has happened to Jesus (who is both divine Lord and human
being), for our sake and to our advantage: 'He was handed over
for our sins and was raised for our justification' (Romans 4.25).

His resurrection, the NT proclaims, has inaugurated the
general resurrection to come at the end (e.g. Romans 8.29; 1
Corinthians 15.20–8). The passage in 1 Corinthians to which
reference has just been made could hardly be clearer about
the risen Jesus and his saving impact on everyone. The One
who does and will do this is the same as the Jesus who was
crucified and is the subject of Paul's preaching (1 Corinthians
1.10–2.2), and certainly not supposed to be the divine Word of
God who has left behind his human being and its properties.

In his glorified humanity, the risen Jesus is the agent (or rather joint agent with the Holy Spirit) through whom human beings will be raised and enjoy divine life for ever. As Karl Rahner puts it, 'the Word – by the fact that he is man and insofar as he is this – is the necessary and permanent mediator of all salvation, not merely at some time in the past but now and for all eternity'.[6]

To sum this up. Without assuming a human nature (in all its bodiliness and freedom), the Son of God could not have lived and realized a human history. Likewise unless he maintained, albeit in a glorified state, his bodily humanity, we could not talk about his resurrection from the dead. But in fact the human condition he assumed at the incarnation persists eternally in his new, exalted state, and does so for the eternal salvation of all human beings. Both in his earthly lifetime and in his risen life, what occurred at the incarnation persists – for the salvation of human beings who are already touched by his power and will meet him in glory when he 'comes to judge the living and the dead'.

Forrest's article suggests that worries about the permanence of the incarnation may derive from some forms of a 'kenotic' or self-emptying interpretation of Christ. If one thinks of the incarnation as abandoning divine powers and, in effect, divinity, then the 'resurrection' will mean abandoning humanity to resume divine powers or divinity. But is this a justifiable way of interpreting the self-emptying or self-limitation of the incarnation? We face this question in a later chapter.

Notes

1.   See M. F. Connell, *'Descensus Christi ad Inferos:* Christ's Descent to the Dead', *Theological Studies* 62 (2001), 262–82.

2.   G. Dix, *The Apostolic Tradition* (London: SPCK, 1968), 7–8.

3.   Karl Adam, *The Christ of Faith* (London: Burns & Oates, 1957), 302.

4. 'The Incarnation: a Philosophical Case for Kenosis', *Religious Studies* 36 (2000), 127–40.

5. That the precise words attributed to the risen Christ were actually spoken by him on the occasion of these Easter encounters would be difficult to argue. What we read are rather words fashioned by the evangelists or drawn from the current practices of their community, such as the trinitarian baptismal formula Matthew puts in Jesus' mouth (Matthew 28.19).

6. See K. Rahner, 'The Eternal Significance of the Humanity of Jesus for our Relationship with God', *Theological Investigations* 3 (London: Darton, Longman & Todd, 1967), 35–46.

4

The Paradox of the Incarnation

Immensity cloistered in thy dear womb. (John Donne, 'Annunciation')

Modernity is not well equipped to understand what lies at the heart of Christian thought, namely the intimacy of eternity and temporality in Jesus Christ. (Gerard Loughlin, 'Time', *The Oxford Companion to Christian Thought*)

The London exhibition 'Seeing Salvation' in the spring of 2000 squarely faced the most difficult task for artists, as well as for preachers, composers, theologians and other writers: how should they represent Christ's two natures or his being both truly divine and fully human? How can the same individual be both divine and human? Divinity and humanity constitute and disclose seemingly incompatible ranges of characteristics. Divinity involves a purely spiritual, all-powerful, all-knowing, omnipresent, eternal and unlimited way of being. Humanity involves a material and temporal existence that is spatially located and limited in power and knowledge. How, then, can one individual possess and disclose these two incompatible ranges of characteristics, and so be simultaneously all-powerful and limited in power, all-knowing and limited in knowledge, eternal and temporal, and so forth? The very notion of incarnation seems to be logically inconceivable, since it attributes to one and the same individual mutually exclusive sets of characteristics.

Two frames of reference

No sensible person can be expected to believe claims that are blatantly contradictory. There is no way, for instance, of showing that it is only apparently contradictory to claim that Luciano is both five feet tall and well over six feet tall. There is a real contradiction here and no explanation will remove the incoherence. As Stephen Davis observes, 'it is never rational under any circumstances to believe a contradiction.'[1]

But does the incarnation claim involve such a blatant contradiction, or is it only a seeming contradiction? A distinction, ultimately rooted in the teaching of the Council of Chalcedon (451), can save the day. This Council called 'our Lord Jesus Christ' 'one in being (*homoousios*) with the Father as to the divinity and one in being with us as to the humanity' (DH 301; ND 614). Then the Chalcedonian definition went on to distinguish between Christ's 'one person' and 'two natures'. Following the distinction drawn between what he is 'as to his divinity' and what he is 'as to his humanity', we may speak of Christ being all-powerful, all-knowing, eternal and infinite by virtue of his divine nature, and being limited in power and knowledge, temporal and finite by virtue of his human nature. Within one frame of reference Christ discloses one range of characteristics; within another frame of reference he discloses another range of characteristics.

It is not that we should hope to establish positively the internal coherence of the incarnation. It remains a central religious mystery, something which we are justified in believing but which we can never expect to comprehend or understand fully. The incarnation claim that the infinite and the finite are united in the one person of Christ is mysterious and paradoxical. But, as I aim to show in a later chapter, we may sensibly accept it.

'Mystery' is to be understood here, not as a merely obscure, puzzling or even inexplicable matter (e.g. the identity of the murderer when the body of some victim is discovered), but rather as a deep, divine truth disclosed through Jesus Christ. Even after it has been revealed, the mysterious reality of God and the divine action for human redemption continue to go beyond the clear grasp of human reason. Ultimately we can speak of only one mystery, that of the tripersonal God who invites us through the Son's saving incarnation and the mission of the Holy Spirit to share the divine life for ever.

I use 'paradox' in the serious sense of something which involves an apparent contradiction, but which in fact is well founded and can be appropriately accepted. Here it applies to the divine mystery of the incarnation. Belief in the incarnation appears to involve the contradiction of attributing to one and the same person two mutually exclusive sets of properties. But, on closer theological inspection and with suitable distinctions, belief in the incarnation can be saved from being dismissed as blatantly incoherent. 'Paradox' is not intended frivolously as in the case of the 'most ingenious paradox' which saves the situation for Frederic in Gilbert and Sullivan's *Pirates of Penzance*. Being born in a leap year on 29 February, he may have lived for 21 years but has missed three out of every four birthdays and so turns out to be 'a little boy of five'.

Paradox and incoherence

From the beginning, numerous Christians frankly admitted the paradox of attributing simultaneously properties of divinity and humanity to the incarnate Word. In his homily 'On the Pasch' St Melito of Sardis in the second century used the creation and the crucifixion to focus the paradox. He spoke of Christ as the divine creator who suffered a shameful human death: 'he who hung up the earth is himself hung up; he who fixed the heavens is himself fixed [on a cross]; he who fastened everything is fastened on the wood; the Master is reviled; God has been killed' (no. 96). Such a belief could not go unchallenged. St Justin Martyr (d. *c.* 165) recorded the baffled reactions of cultured Jews of his time. Their monotheistic faith and sense of God's infinite 'otherness' made it quite 'incredible' and 'impossible' for them to think of God deigning to be born of a human being and end up dying on a cross (*Dialogue with Trypho*, 68). A few years later Origen (d. *c.* 254) responded to similar scepticism over the incarnation coming from Celsus, a learned pagan who had declared God to be 'incapable' of incarnation; divinity, being immortal and immutable, and humanity could not be united in the one Christ (*Contra Celsum*, 4.14). The very notion of incarnation seemed to push beyond the merely paradoxical and embody logically incoherent ideas.

The charge that faith in the incarnate Word involves an incoherent claim has flared up right down to our own day. In the nineteenth century F. D. E. Schleiermacher framed the issue this way: 'one individual cannot share in two quite different natures'.[2] In the twentieth century Don Cupitt put the same objection even more vigorously: 'the eternal God and an historical man are two beings of quite different ontological status. It is quite unintelligible to declare them identical'.[3] One could multiply examples of those who detect in the notion of incarnation mutually exclusive properties and so conclude that the incarnation is simply incoherent in itself.

I offered above one response to this difficulty – in terms of different frames of reference. If we distinguish between the incarnate Son of God *inasmuch* as he is human and *inasmuch* as he is divine, we go some distance in delivering belief in the incarnation from being proved to be essentially incoherent.

This belief is not blatantly incoherent like talk of a married bachelor or a square circle.

One could add a further, important point here. It is often extremely difficult to prove something to be either coherent or incoherent. In the case of the incarnation, we face not only the question of divinity and humanity belonging coherently together (or not doing so), but also the question of the coherence of the two components, especially the coherence of the first component: our notion of divinity. No direct proof for the coherence of the concept of God can be offered. On the contrary, many thinkers continue to find the massive presence of terrible evil in our world a decisive argument against admitting the existence of an all-powerful, all-loving and all-knowing God. If it is very difficult or even impossible to prove directly the coherence of the concept of God, no one can be expected to establish the coherence of the claim that divinity and humanity are united in the person of Jesus Christ. In other words, arguments about the coherence or incoherence of the incarnation presuppose necessarily that we have some well-thought-out position about the coherence or incoherence of what it is like to be God.

The situation, then, for a debate about the coherence or incoherence of the very notion of the incarnation is very different from any talk of a square circle or a married bachelor. Our clear ideas about the four-sided nature of squares and circles having all their points equidistant from the centre let us see at once that a geometrical figure cannot be simultaneously a square and a circle. The definition of terms rules out talk of a 'married bachelor': someone's marital status cannot simultaneously be that of being married and unmarried (or not yet married). One might justify this expression by explaining: 'the man did go through a marriage ceremony in his college chapel, but he remains at heart a bachelor don of the worst kind'. But then, of course, one is using 'married' in the literal sense, but 'bachelor' in an extended sense and no longer in a literal sense.

In the case of the coherence or incoherence of the incarnation, we have nothing like such a clear understanding of the two components involved. How do we know what properties are essential to being God and to being human? Our limited ideas about what God and we ourselves are like seem to stand in the way of declaring or denying that an incarnation is coherent and possible. Of course, once we agree that the Son of God did become incarnate in Jesus of Nazareth, we must also agree that incarnation is possible and coherent. For believers, the fact of the incarnation automatically establishes its possibility and coherence.

Coming to believe in the incarnation requires, however, some provisional knowledge of divine and human characteristics. If we are going to recognize Jesus as the 'God-man', we need to know something about the basic properties of God and human beings. Our belief in the incarnate Word of God will undoubtedly cause us to revise that prior knowledge. However, at least logically some 'prior' knowledge of divine and human characteristics must come into play if we are to confess: 'Truly this man is the Son of God.' A later chapter will develop this issue when examining the credibility of faith in the incarnation.

Poems, paintings and hymns

At the end of the day, poets, painters and hymn-writers offer us more help towards appreciating with amazed wonder the paradox of Jesus being simultaneously truly divine and fully human. As the woman from whom he drew his humanity, Jesus' mother features prominently in very many of these artistic approaches.

Dante Alighieri (1265–1321) places his classic tribute to Mary at the start of Canto 33 of *Paradiso*, the closing canto of the whole *Divine Comedy*. In addressing her as 'Virgin, yet a Mother, Daughter of thy Son', he moves from the mysterious truth of her as a virgin conceiving Jesus to the paradox of her being created by the One to whom she gave birth.

John Donne (1573–1631) also focuses the mysterious union in Christ of divinity and humanity through the paradox of Mary being the human maker of her Maker and the mother of her Father, with Christ understood to be 'father', as in Edward Caswall's hymn.[4] Donne's poem 'Annunciation' revelled in the paradox of the Infinite Son of God accepting a finite existence through the incarnation. Before time was created, the One whom Mary was to conceive in time had conceived her in the divine mind and intentions. After his human conception, the Light of the world was shut up and confined within the holy but dark cloister of Mary's womb.

> Salvation to all that will is nigh,
> That All, which always is All everywhere,
> Which cannot sin, and yet all sins must bear,
> Which cannot die, yet cannot choose but die,
> Lo, faithful Virgin, yields himself to lie
> In prison, in thy womb; and though he there
> Can take no sin, nor thou give, yet he will wear
> Taken from thence, flesh, which death's force may try.
> Ere by the spheres time was created, thou
> Wast in his mind, who is thy Son and Brother,
> Whom thou conceiv'st, conceived; yea thou are now
> Thy Maker's maker, and thy Father's mother,
> Thou hast light in dark; and shutst in little room,
> Immensity cloistered in thy dear womb.

Rather than playing with the paradox of Mary being her 'Maker's maker' and her 'Father's mother', W. H. Auden suggested that the salvation of mortal, human beings requires an 'impossible miracle'. We can be saved only by the miraculous power entailed in the paradox of the Eternal One acting in time and the Infinite One becoming finite. In *For the Time Being: A Christmas Oratio* Auden wrote:

> We who must die demand a miracle.
> How could the Eternal do a temporal act,
> The Infinite become a finite fact?
> Nothing can save us that is possible:
> We who must die demand a miracle.

Painters have often moved beyond the annunciation and the conception of Christ to focus on the union of divinity and humanity revealed at his nativity. They meet the challenge of depicting together the two natures by expressing their faith through the visual, narrative forms which Christmas continues to keep very familiar.

Thus artists have pictured the shepherds who are prompted by angels to visit the newly born Jesus and offer him divine worship. Painters have repeatedly drawn from Luke's narrative this adoration by the shepherds, so as to give visual form to Jesus' humanity and divinity: the former comes through the baby's obvious helplessness and vulnerability, the latter through the posture of the shepherds who adore him.

From the time Christian funerary art started in the catacombs of Rome, believers repeatedly turned to Matthew's story of the Magi travelling from afar to worship the child Jesus. In the Epiphany paintings we see the representatives of the people of the world arriving to adore the newly born divine King. The Magi worship the divine Christ at his humble coming into the world, even as all believers will greet him in his divine glory when he comes at the end in judgement. The Magi, whom artists and others soon raised to royal status, recognize in the Christ Child not just a king, but the King of kings, the divine sovereign of the universe.

At times painters have used Mary and Joseph to put into focus the mysterious union of divinity and humanity in the child Jesus. One of the last works by the seventeenth-century Spanish painter Murillo, 'The Heavenly and Earthly Trinities', shows the earthly trinity of Jesus, Mary and Joseph, which intersects in the figure of Jesus with the celestial Trinity of Father, Son and Holy Spirit. The Christ Child stands on a cornerstone, which lifts him above his human parents and allows them to kneel and worship him. Sometimes dismissed as too sentimental, this crowning work by Murillo functions extremely well to portray the personal union of humanity and divinity in Christ.

When facing the union of the divine and human in Christ, poets and painters are not content with simply showing their skills in dealing with a merely intellectual challenge, as regrettably theologians and philosophers sometimes seem to do. The verbal and visual images which they produce show poets and painters aiming to change the lives of their audiences. They do this best when working with the first and last stages of Jesus' life, his humble birth and terrible death – episodes that stretch the tension between his divinity and humanity almost to breaking point. The Christ Child's humanity is beyond question; he needs nurture, protection and affection to survive and grow. The crucified Jesus' humanity is also beyond question, as he dies in excruciating agony. Faith invites us to recognize also the true divinity of the One who is unquestionably human. Where theology may make the union of humanity and divinity in Christ complex, painted and verbal images make faith in the God-man accessible and attractive.

Right from the time of the NT, hymns have rendered the paradox of the incarnation intelligible and convincing – not least, those hymns which centre on the birth of Jesus or on his death and resurrection. By imaginatively evoking feelings, the best of Christmas carols can initiate and nourish faith in the union in Christ of humanity and divinity. The second verse of Charles Wesley's 'Hark, the herald angels sing' joyfully encourages such faith:

> Veiled in flesh the Godhead see,
> hail the incarnate Deity!
> Pleased as man with man to dwell,
> Jesus, our Emmanuel.

'Once in royal David's city', another much-loved Christmas carol, calls forth tender amazement at the Son of God's loving self-abasement in the incarnation:

> He came down to earth from heaven,
> who is God and Lord of all,
> and his shelter was a stable
> and his cradle was a stall;
> with the poor, and mean, and lowly,
> lived on earth our Saviour holy.

In a 'High Mass' the Credo has offered composers the chance of expressing the mysterious union in Christ of humanity and divinity, especially in the settings they create for the words, 'and he became flesh from the Holy Spirit and the Virgin Mary, and was made man (*et incarnatus est de Spiritu Sancto ex Maria Virgine et homo factus est)*'. At that point in the Credo but also throughout his B Minor Mass, Johann Sebastian Bach (d. 1750), with intense and effective faith, communicated the mystery of the incarnation.[5]

Hymns that focus on the Son of God's humiliation in crucifixion can also communicate a deep sense of what the incarnation led to and meant. Take, for instance, the hymn composed, or perhaps taken over, by St Paul for his Letter to the Philippians (2.6–11). This hymn, sung or recited in the

Divine Office of the Western Church at vespers every Saturday evening, brings into focus the death on the cross. The One who was 'in the form of God' truly assumed 'the form of a slave' in taking on the human condition and ending his life on a cross. God (the Father) responded to his Son's humble obedience by highly exalting him and giving him the divine name of *Kyrios* (Lord). With his divinity now disclosed to all creatures, the glorified Jesus receives divine honour from the universe. Far from being the mere apotheosis of some hero rewarded with divinity for a job well done (as in so many non-Christian legends), the unquestioned divine identity of the Son (Philippians 2.6) is now revealed through his glorious exaltation from death. In the form of the antiphon *Christus factus est pro nobis obediens* ('Christ became obedient for us'), Paul's poignant hymn has been chanted for over 1,000 years and proved itself highly effective in communicating and illuminating belief in Jesus as both truly divine and fully human.

Paul's verb for expressing the incarnation, 'he emptied himself' (Philippians 2.7) has given rise to much literature about the kenotic self-limitation of the incarnation. To that issue we turn in the next chapter.

Notes

1. 'John Hick on Incarnation and Trinity', in S. Davis, D. Kendall and G. O'Collins (eds), *The Trinity* (Oxford: Oxford University Press, 1999), 251–72, at 258.
2. *The Christian Faith* (Edinburgh: T. & T. Clark, 1928), 393.
3. 'The Finality of Christ', *Theology* 78 (1975), 618–28, at 625.
4. Caswall's translation from the *Catholicum Hymnologium Germanicum* ran as follows: 'To Christ, the prince of peace,/And Son of God most high,/The father of the world to come,/Sing we with holy joy.' Putting *father* here in lower-case and immediately after Christ being named as *Son of God most high* respects the technical trinitarian sense of *Father* (upper-case). The lines also echo

what is said in Isaiah 9.6 about 'the child born to us', who will be named *Everlasting Father* and *Prince of Peace*.

5.   See W. Mellers, 'Bach, Johann Sebastian', *The Oxford Companion to Christian Thought*, 57–8.

The Self-limitation of the Incarnation

Suppose then a king who loved a humble maiden.
(Soren Kierkegaard, *Philosophical Fragments*)

There is an infinite difference between the power and
knowledge of the pre-incarnate Word and the powerlessness and ignorance of Jesus at birth. (Peter Forrest,
'The Incarnation: a Philosophical Case for Kenosis')

'What did the incarnation do to God?' This insightful
question, recently put to me by a cherished friend, Norman
Young, opens up valuable trains of thought. One can rephrase
the question in terms of St Paul's language in Philippians 2:
of what did the Son of God 'empty' or divest himself in the
incarnation? Let us begin with a parable, the most famous
parable of all those elaborated by Soren Kierkegaard, 'The
King and the Maiden'.[1]

The king and the maiden

In his parable which, as he admits, sounds like a fairy tale,
Kierkegaard imagines a maiden who belongs to the poorest
class and lives in the most deprived circumstances. A
powerful and noble-minded king falls in love with her. He is
troubled by the question: 'Would she be happy to live at his

side? Could she summon up enough confidence never to
remember what the king would wish only to forget: that he is
king and she has been a humble maiden?' 'Even if',
Kierkegaard continues, 'the maiden would be content to
become as nothing, this could not satisfy the king, precisely
because he loves her, and because it is harder for him to be
her benefactor than to lose her.'

Kierkegaard applies his parable to God, who is driven by
love to reveal himself and to 'win' the human 'learner'. In and
through love 'the unequal can be made equal'; and in and
through this 'equality or unity . . . an understanding can be
effected'. But, without 'annihilating the unlikeness that
exists between them', how is God going to overcome the
infinite difference and 'make himself understood'?

Or, to return to the king, how could the love between the
king and the maiden be made a truly happy love without any
deception or delusion entering in? It would be terrible deception, Kierkegaard observes, to 'elevate' abruptly the humble
maiden and let her suddenly find her 'fortune made'. The
'tumultuous joy' of such an outward change would deceive the
king's own heart and the maiden herself. Or perhaps the king
might 'show himself to the humble maiden in all the pomp of
his power, causing the sun of his presence to rise over her
cottage, shedding a glory over the scene, and making her
forget herself in worshipful admiration'. This might 'satisfy
the maiden, but it could not satisfy the king'. After all, he
desires 'not his glorification but hers'. He cannot deceive her;
to express imperfectly his love for her would be 'in his
eyes a deception'. Union, Kierkegaard concludes, 'must be
attempted by a descent'.

The parable thus reaches this point: for union to be
brought about, love must 'alter itself'. God must become our
equal and 'appear in the likeness of the humblest' and 'in the
form of a servant'. Both for God and for the king, 'the unfath-
omable nature of love . . . desires equality with the beloved'.

In God's case omnipotent love 'is able to accomplish its purpose' – something that the king could not do. His 'beggar-cloak' will 'flutter loosely about him' and betray him. In the case of the incarnate Son of God his 'servant-form is no mere outer garment'. He 'must suffer all things, endure all things, make experience of all things. He must suffer hunger in the desert, he must thirst in the time of his agony, he must be forsaken in death.'

Kierkegaard's answer to the question 'What did the incarnation do to God?' echoes, of course, what St Paul wrote in Philippians 2.6–11 about Jesus Christ who, 'being first in the form of God', took 'the form of a servant' and 'emptied himself' in his incarnation. The One who 'did not think his being equal to God something to be exploited' to his own advantage, became human and 'obedient to death, even death on a cross'. The apostle Paul underlines here the terrifying contrast between the state of 'being equal to God' and 'dying on a cross'.

Unlike Kierkegaard's parable, Paul's hymn does not explicitly mention the love which drove the Son of God to descend, take the form of a servant, and even suffer death to bring about union with us. Other letters of the apostle celebrate that unconditional love (e.g. Romans 5.6–11; Galatians 2.20). The Philippians hymn sets out starkly what the incarnation did to the Son of God and where his self-emptying brought him – to the cross on Calvary. The reader may long for this hymn to recognize Christ's self-sacrificing love. The fact that Paul leaves that love unsaid works to underline it even more. Kierkegaard's parable makes explicit the love that motivated the self-abasement that constituted the incarnation. Kierkegaard drives home this point with the question that forms the subtitle of the parable: 'To what shall we compare the divine love that overcomes the infinite distance between human sin and the holiness of God?'

Paul's meaning

Kierkegaard's parable has won wide acceptance and admiration. But not all readings of Paul's hymn have been welcomed. Before coming to questions raised by various 'kenotic' theories, let me set out the biblical exposition that I would support.[2] Some exegetes unpack verse 6 in human terms and as a comparison between Christ and Adam. Even though Paul writes of 'Christ Jesus' as being 'in the form of God', such exegetes want to take this as equivalent to the language of Adam and Eve being created 'in the image' and 'after the likeness of God' (Genesis 1.26–7). (This is a thoroughly questionable claim, since Paul would have introduced 'image' and/or 'likeness' if he wanted his readers to recall the Genesis story.) Then these exegetes argue that the 'becoming *like* God himself' in the serpent's temptation (Genesis 3.5–6, 22) is equivalent to the 'being *equal* to God' of Christ's opening state in Paul's hymn. Adam and Eve succumbed to the temptation and tried to become like God by seizing the fruit which was not yet in their hands, whereas the man Jesus made no such wrongful attempt to seize a share in divinity. But once again the alleged equivalence remains dubious: equality and likeness are not the same and would not have been so understood by Paul's readers.

The exegesis that introduces Adam and Eve understands *harpagmos*, a word which occurs only here in the NT, as meaning 'something to be seized' or 'taken possession of'. The translation of the New Revised Standard Version strikes me as much more convincing: 'something to be exploited'. What did Christ, who was already 'in the form' or mode of being of God, have to seize? Nothing. The picture rather is that of Someone who belongs by right to the sphere of God but does not want to exploit or retain egoistically or to his own advantage his divine prerogatives and privileges.

In short, verse 6 presents Christ's divine existence and

status prior to his assuming the human condition. With its emphatic, initial 'but', verse 7 brings us to 'the form of a servant' and his 'being born in human likeness' and 'being found in the human condition'. It is here in verse 7 that the humanity inherited from Adam and Eve turns up, yet does so with 'the form of a servant' clearly opposed to 'the form of God' of verse 6 and with the 'being born in human likeness' which implies that he was not so before.

The question then becomes: what is involved in One who is in the form of God taking on the form of a human servant or slave? In the context of the hymn this turns into the question: what does 'he emptied himself' (v. 7) mean? Does it mean literally stripping himself of the form or mode of being of God, not merely surrendering for the duration of Christ's earthly life the exercise of divine power and the revelation of divine glory but literally relinquishing, at least for a time, some or even all of the divine attributes (e.g. being all-powerful and all-knowing) and temporarily not possessing them? Let me delay for the moment any answers to these questions, and note how part of what is involved emerges from what follows after 'he emptied himself': first, three participles ('taking the form of a servant', 'being born in human likeness' and 'being found in the human condition'); and then the terrifying verb, 'he humbled himself', explained as 'becoming obedient to the point of death, even death on a cross'. As a radical sign of one's being truly human, death takes away any suspicion that the 'being born in human likeness' means not a genuine likeness but only a mere likeness, as if he only appeared to be human but was not truly so. Through his own initiative, Christ comes to be 'in the form' or authentically human mode of being, just as he is 'in the form' or mode of being of God.

Self-limitation

In and of itself, Paul's cryptic 'he emptied himself' will not help us much in answering the hard questions posed in the last paragraph. Answers here will depend on our view of God, put together from the Scriptures, the Christian tradition, the insights of philosophers, and our own personal experience of God.

At the very least, the divine choice to be embodied and to be 'found in the human condition' necessarily involved the willingness to assume certain limitations. In deciding to live also as a human being, the Son of God took on new but limited powers and new but limited ways of acting. In his human condition he would depend on physical factors and so experience finite limits: for instance, his ability to think humanly would depend upon a healthy, intact and consciously awake brain. Being human entails being limited and dependent in a whole range of physical and psychological ways.

The most startling self-limitations of the incarnation are located at the beginning and at the end of the Son of God's human story. Both before and after birth one cannot overlook his vulnerability and dependence on others, above all on his mother. He could not have survived and grown without her. Then, at the end his brutal death by crucifixion puts before our eyes a victim of human violence and sin who seems powerless to defend himself.

Since the nineteenth century some writers have proposed that the 'self-emptying' of the incarnation entailed the Son of God temporarily abdicating some or even all of the normal divine powers and properties, only to resume them again at the end of his earthly life. He became truly human by ceasing to be (actually) divine. A more cautious version of the 'self-emptying' holds that the Son of God, while continuing to possess divine powers, did not exercise them (or did not exercise all of them) during the years of his 'kenotic', human existence. There is, so one can argue, a distinction to be drawn between possessing some properties and exercising them; a superb pianist can take a holiday and need not perform every day.

The former view notoriously runs up against serious objections. Can one member of the Trinity, even by free choice, become bereft of his divine powers? Surely properties that belong essentially to God cannot be abandoned, even for a moment? Such a change appears to conflict with God being intrinsically and essentially unchangeable. A change like this would seem to spell the end of divine life for the Son of God. If the second person of the Trinity ceases to have divine powers, he would cease to be God. But can a divine person cease to be divine?

Second, Archbishop William Temple issued a famous challenge to the strong kenotic theory in the form of a rhetorical question: 'What was happening to the rest of the universe during the period of our Lord's earthly life?'[3] How could the cosmos survive if the Word of God who keeps it in existence divested himself for a time of his creative and conserving power? The more radical question, however, is: what happens to God if this could occur? The idea of one person of the Trinity divesting himself of his divine powers seems to imply tritheism, or a belief in 'three gods' who do not share the one divinity but function together in perfect harmony. At the incarnation, one of these 'three gods' is supposed to relinquish for a time omnipotence and other divine attributes, leaving the other two divine persons to carry on the business of keeping in existence the whole universe. Thus, strong forms of kenoticism seem to dissolve the unity of the one God into tritheism, or acceptance of 'three gods' each with its own nature, being or substance.

Third, if the Son of God abdicates his divine powers for a time, what stops him from doing so permanently? If there are good reasons for temporarily abdicating such powers, there could be such reasons for permanently abdicating them. Fourth, if one member of the Trinity abdicates for a time his divine powers, why stop there? Surely then, all three persons of the Trinity could do so, and, one might imagine, do so at the same time? What happens then to the continuous divine activity needed to keep the created world in existence? Some defenders of a kenotic view that involves giving up divine powers argue at this point that only the second person of the Trinity could become incarnate – a view to which we return in a later chapter. If incarnation with its attendant self-emptying of divine powers is a possibility for only one divine person, the other two divine persons – the kenoticists maintain – retain and exercise their divine powers, e.g. for the conservation of the universe. Fifth, there is a problem about the permanence of the incarnation. Some kenoticists postulate this sequence: at the incarnation the divine powers are abandoned and the human condition assumed; after his death the Son of God resumes his divine powers but abandons his humanity. Such a loss of humanity is incompatible with the permanence of the incarnation for which Chapter 3 argued.

The more cautious form of kenoticism, divine powers being possessed but not exercised, looks attractive at first glance. The difficulty, however, with the analogies proposed, such as that of the great pianist who does not necessarily perform all the time, comes from the fact that such analogies involve powers that are acquired and cultivated through practice. It seems very difficult to imagine God acquiring new powers and cultivating them through practice. Every divine power, such as being all-powerful and all-knowing, belongs to God necessarily.[4]

Furthermore, in its prudent teaching about the Son of God assuming the human condition, the Council of Chalcedon declared that the properties or essential features of both the divine and the human nature are *preserved* in the incarnation (DH 302; ND 615). This teaching seems to rule out even a cautious form of kenotic theory, which proposes that the divine properties were, at least temporarily, not preserved after the incarnation, or at least not preserved in action.

What might one propose then about the powers possessed and exercised by the incarnate Son of God? Can we suggest anything that could spell out Paul's language of 'self-emptying'? It seems appropriate to distinguish, without separating them, a three-fold exercise of powers during the earthly life of Jesus. First, as the second person of the Trinity he does not take some kind of sabbatical leave from the exercise of divine powers; together with the Father and the Holy Spirit he continues, for example, the divine work of conserving in existence the created universe. Second, there are mixed activities, for instance, Christ's miraculous works. These involved the divine actions that went beyond God's normal activity in the world. But they also involved human words and gestures on the part of Jesus, when – for instance – he touched the skin of lepers or the eyes of the blind and verbalized his desire to heal them. In such cases Christ used both his human resources and his divine power. Third, some actions entail only the exercise of human powers: as when, for instance, Christ ate, drank, wept, took children in his arms, proclaimed his message of the kingdom and chose a core group of twelve disciples. Some of these human operations, such as, for example, falling asleep through sheer weariness and being terribly distressed during prayer in the garden of Gethsemane, highlight the humble, servant role taken on by the One who emptied and limited himself for our sake. Unless he had emptied himself, he could never have wept, fallen asleep or prayed in fearful distress. Paul's hymn and Kierkegaard's parable invite us to remember and cherish the love showed by the divine King in assuming the limited and painful operations and sufferings of our human condition.

Kierkegaard compared the divine love at work in the incarnation with that of a powerful king being ready to 'disguise himself' as a lowly servant. Georges Rouault (1871–1938) went further – by portraying Jesus as a clown. Our terrible need drove the Son of God to 'empty himself' by becoming a weak and foolish buffoon. His incautious and even preposterous love led him to the final 'foolishness' of death on a cross.

Notes

1. Trans. W. Lowrie, in T. C. Oden (ed.), *Parables of Kierkegaard* (Princeton: Princeton University Press, 1978), 40–5.
2. The commentators on Philippians from whom I have drawn most help include: J.-N. Aletti, B. Byrne, G. D. Fee, J. Gnilka, J. Heriban, R. P. Martin, P. T. O'Brien and N. T. Wright.
3. *Christus Veritas* (London: Macmillan, 1924), 142.
4. For literature on kenotic theories of the incarnation, see C. S. Evans, 'The Self-Emptying of Love: Some Thoughts on Kenotic Christology', in S. Davis, D. Kendall and G. O'Collins (eds), *The Incarnation* (Oxford: Oxford University Press, 2002), 246–72; and P. Forrest, 'The Incarnation: a Philosophical Case for Kenosis', *Religious Studies* 36 (2000), 127–40.

6

One Person in Two Natures

Love does not alter the beloved, it alters itself. (Soren Kierkegaard, 'The King and the Maiden')

We are steeped in an intellectual heritage which ... has agreed with Aquinas in according supreme value to personhood, but accounts for this in terms of self-consciousness and the capacity for relationship rather than metaphysical status. (Hugh Pyper, 'Person', *The Oxford Companion to Christian Thought*)

How far does the humble 'descent' of the Son of God go – to draw further on Kierkegaard's parable? If love 'alters itself', what 'alteration' does the incarnation bring to the Son of God?

Chalcedon

The teaching of the Council of Chalcedon (AD 451) about one person or subsistence (*hypostasis*) in two natures has remained normative for mainstream Christianity. It was here that the Council made its most important contribution: an official and standard terminology about the incarnate Son of God. We return below to a key question: how well have the terms 'person' and 'natures' worn over more than fifteen centuries? For the moment let me simply note that *hypostasis* as signifying one individual had and has a wider application than 'person' as signifying a rational individual. Every person is an *hypostasis*, but not every *hypostasis* (e.g. an individual dog or tree) is a person. One might sum up the specific contribution of Chalcedonian teaching by saying that the incarnate Word of God is only one individual but has two 'things', his divine and human natures. He is one 'who' but has two 'whats'. The 'oneness' we acknowledge with reference to the person, and the 'twoness' with reference to the natures.

Hence the incarnate Son of God is and was a human being (or better, has and had a full human nature), but is not a human person. He took on or assumed all the natural endowments of a human being, but did not become a human person. In addition to the characteristics of divinity that he already possessed from eternity, the Word of God acquired around 5 BC all the essential characteristics of a human being. That made him, and continues to make him, a genuine human being. His loving 'descent' from heaven 'altered' him by adding the human nature through which he could operate visibly. But his humanity did not and does not have the independence that would constitute a second (human) person alongside the divine person of the Word of God.

If in the incarnation the Son of God had, so to speak, 'teamed up with' an already existing person, he would not truly have 'become flesh' (John 1.14) or assumed the full human condition (Philippians 2.7–8). What would have resulted would have been a very special, even uniquely special, relationship between two individuals: a divine subject (the person of the Son of God) and a human subject (the person of the Son of Mary), who would be very intimately related to the Son of God but not strictly identical with him. Any such 'two-sons' view in effect excludes a genuine incarnation and pictures Christ as a kind of temple of the divine Word or as a person filled with the divine Spirit.[1] Such a

Christ might differ in degree from others so graced by God, but not in kind.

Natures and person

As has normally been the case with general councils of the Church, the Council of Chalcedon used the terms 'natures' (*physeis*) and 'person' (*prosopon*) or 'subsistence' (*hypostasis*), without stopping to define them. What is 'two' in Christ, it called the natures, what (or rather who) is 'one' it called the person or subsistence. Instead of being the proper work of an ecumenical council, the analysis and definition of terms belong rather to philosophers and theologians.

Prosopon, after initially indicating a mask worn by an actor on stage to signify some character, began to denote the visible manifestation or 'face' of someone – in a sense, someone's public 'persona'. Without too much trouble, through the third into the fifth century *'prosopon'* or 'persona' came to indicate an individual human being, while still maintaining the overtones of such an individual as visibly manifested.

For centuries, however, *hypostasis* was dogged by controversy, in particular when translated into Latin as *'sub-stantia'* or 'that which stands under'. To begin with, *hypostasis* could, among other things, denote either an 'essence', that is to say, a (common) substance in the usual Latin sense, or an 'individuating principle'. Almost inevitably, therefore, St Dionysius of Rome (d. 268) was scandalized by Christians in Alexandria using Origen's terminology about the Trinity and speaking of three *hypostaseis* in God. The Pope took this to be an heretical doctrine of three divine substances or three divinities (DH 112; ND 301).

The ambiguity for Romans in the meaning of the Greek *hypostasis*, either substance/essence or subject/person, emerged in a furiously indignant letter from St Jerome

(*c.* 345–420) to Pope Damasus. About 30 years of age, Jerome
was then living among some hermits in the Middle East. He
had met some Greek-speaking Christians who shocked him
by their terminology for the Trinity:

> [They] are trying to extort from me, a Roman Christian,
> their unheard-of formula of 'three hypostases' . . . I ask
> them what 'three hypostases' are supposed to mean.
> They reply, 'three persons subsisting'. I rejoin that this
> is my belief. They are not satisfied with the meaning;
> they demand the term. (*Epistola*, 15.3)

Less than a century later, however, by endorsing the teaching
of Chalcedon, St Leo the Great (Pope 440–51) and Latin
Christians did just what had outraged Jerome: they accepted
hypostasis as meaning a subsisting subject rather than the
basic essence or substance.

The Chalcedonian definition obviously took the two
'natures' as equivalent to (a) 'divinity' and 'humanity', to (b)
being 'truly God' and 'truly man', or to (c) being as God
homoousios (of the same substance) with the Father and as
man *homoousios* (of the same substance) with us. In the case
of the 'consubstantiality' with the Father, the Council had in
mind a numerically identical substance or being. Here it
understood 'same' in the sense of identical; there is only one
divine substance. But in the case of 'consubstantiality' with
us, the Council used the term in a generic sense. There are
innumerable instances of the human substance or being. We
share the 'same' substance with Christ, but we do not share
an 'identical' substance with him. Our being is not 'one and
the same', individual substance with his.

By supplying right at the heart of its special contribution
to teaching on Christ three sets of equivalents for 'two
natures' (see (a), (b) and (c) above), Chalcedon refrained from
rigidly imposing just one way of speaking about the duality in

Christ. The principal churches in both East and West accepted the language of 'one person' in 'two natures', but some groups of Christians would not do so and at times suffered for not endorsing the complete Chalcedonian teaching. Better relations between Christian communities in the twentieth century have led to agreements about faith in Jesus Christ which followed Chalcedon but, out of respect for certain religious and cultural sensitivities, avoided some of the Council's terminology. Thus the May 1973 christological declaration signed by the (Oriental Orthodox) Coptic Pope, Shenouda III of Egypt, and Pope Paul VI of Rome officially set at rest one cause of a schism that went back to 451 when some Christians in Egypt and elsewhere refused to accept the language of 'two natures'. The 1973 declaration avoided that language, but said what is functionally the equivalent by confessing Jesus as 'perfect God with respect to his divinity, perfect man with respect to his humanity'. The declaration went on to say: 'in him are preserved all the properties of the divinity and all the properties of the humanity together in a real, perfect, indivisible and inseparable union' (ND 671a). Thus the declaration could say what Chalcedon taught by using the Chalcedonian God-man and divinity-humanity language.

Down through the centuries the overwhelming majority of Christians repeated Chalcedon's language about the 'two natures' of Christ. At times they forgot the infinite qualitative difference between the uncreated divine nature and the created human nature, falling into the mistake of treating the two natures as if they were two of the same kind or two more or less equal species of the same genus, 'nature'. But until recent times the language of 'two natures' enjoyed almost untroubled possession.

Some modern authors claim that this term has changed or enlarged its meaning too much to be any longer serviceable. What people in the twenty-first century mean by 'nature' is not what the bishops at Chalcedon meant in the fifth century. Unquestionably 'nature' is used in a variety of ways nowadays: as denoting, for example, scenery and countryside (e.g. 'I love walking in the woods and getting back to nature'), or as denoting the universe (e.g. 'The laws of nature apply throughout the cosmos'). But modern languages also still use 'nature' in the sense of the essential features or properties of something – a usage which stands in continuity with Chalcedon's teaching about 'the character proper to each nature' of Christ (DH 302; ND 615) and finds an echo in the 1973 declaration which speaks of 'all the properties' of the divinity and the humanity. The problem is not so much with Chalcedon's two-nature talk (which remains useful and intelligible), but with its teaching of one 'person'.[2]

In the third century Tertullian had written of 'three persons in one substance' to account for the unity and three-ness of God. 'Person' pointed to the distinctive identity of the Father, Son and Holy Spirit – an identity in a dynamic, living relationship derived from one source (the Father), as Tertullian's trinitarian images of the fountain, the river and the canal, or the root, the shoot and the fruit, suggest. St Augustine of Hippo (354–430) conceived of the relations between the three divine persons in terms of the psychological analogy of human memory, understanding and will. At the same time, he recognized 'the great poverty from which our language suffers'. 'The formula of three persons', he pointed out, 'has been coined not in order to give a complete explanation by means of it, but in order that we might not be obliged to remain silent' (*De Trinitate*, 5.10). Up to the time of Augustine, Christians developed their thinking about 'person' in order to frame their doctrine of the Trinity. By the time of Chalcedon, the challenge for teaching and terminology concerned rather the one subject or person, who is Jesus Christ.

More than a half-century after Chalcedon, Boethius (d. *c.* 524) in a work which was also entitled 'On the Person and

Two Natures of Christ' defined 'person' as 'an individual substance of rational nature' (no. 3). This influential account of 'person' highlighted the individuality and rationality of the reality that is the centre of action and attribution. Boethius' rational individual is the 'someone' who acts and who is also the subject to whom we attribute things. But this definition had nothing as such to say about the loving freedom, inter-relatedness and dignity of persons. Medieval theology modified Boethius' account of 'person' by introducing 'existence' (or 'ex-istence' as a loving inter-relatedness that goes out of oneself), and adding the characteristic of incommunicability. In their loving relationships, persons exist in their unique and incommunicable selves. Thus Richard of St Victor defined 'person' as 'the incommunicable ex-istence of an intelligent nature' (*De Trinitate*, 4.22.24). But, especially in the context of his reflections on the Trinity, Richard also emphasized love as central to understanding persons. To be perfect, mutual love must be shared with a third person. The 'personal ideal', realized supremely in the relationship between the three divine persons, is the movement from self-love to mutual love, and then on to shared love. The human dialogue of mutual love must be open and, in fact, shared by a third; the love of two persons is thus fused by a third.

Thomas Aquinas added some footnotes, as it were, to Boethius' notion of person – in particular, about the supreme value of personhood. What proved more decisive, or at least more challenging, was the way René Descartes (1596–1650) furthered the notion of person as a unique subject of consciousness and self-consciousness. More than a century later, a concern for freedom and morality prompted Immanuel Kant (1726–1804) to stress 'person' as the subject of freedom, a moral end in itself, and never a means to an end – a view which recalls Aquinas' stress on the unique dignity of persons. Their different justification for this dignity kept Aquinas and Kant significantly apart. Where Aquinas based personal dignity on God, who regards human beings 'with the greatest respect' (*Summa contra Gentiles*, 3.112), Kant argued that the very nature of persons 'marks them out as ends in themselves' and beings to be treated with dignity and 'never simply as means' (*Groundwork of the Metaphysic of Morals*, 65–6). The philosophical input from Descartes, Kant and John Locke (1632–1704) led to the emergence of a (but not *the*) typically modern notion of person as the subject of self-awareness and freedom – in brief, person as the self-sufficient Ego or the conscious and autonomous self ('I think and am free; therefore I am a person').

From Chalcedon to Boethius, there is a good deal of common ground in the notion of 'person' as a rational, subsisting subject. But the move from Chalcedon's usage of '*prosopon*' and '*hypostasis*' to modern times seems a giant leap. Nowadays many highlight the inter-relatedness of persons; to be a person is to be related to other persons. Persons, if you like, are interpersonal. One could, however, reach back behind Chalcedon to the fourth century and the teaching of the Capaddocian Fathers (St Basil the Great, St Gregory of Nazianzus and St Gregory of Nyssa). Their teaching on the Trinity, which paved the way for the fuller version of the Nicene Creed professed by the First Council of Constantinople and endorsed at Chalcedon, shows a strong sense of persons being interpersonal and in communion. It can well be argued that their understanding of '*hypostasis*' and '*prosopon*' anticipated something of a modern stress on the inter-relatedness of persons.

Much more problematic is a widespread identification of persons with minds. One could say that such a modern equation does no more than push Chalcedon's teaching on Christ's 'rational soul' (DH 301; ND 614) to an extreme. If so, it does this in a way that would be excluded by Chalcedon. If to be a person is to be a mind or conscious self, then Christ's human mind entails his being a distinct human person. With such a move, we would be endorsing something excluded by Chalcedon: two distinct (or even separate?) persons, one human (corresponding to his human mind) and one divine (corresponding to his divine mind) in Christ. This is not to deny that being 'minded' should belong essentially to any account of what it is to be a person or what a person has. What is being challenged is the simple equation: to be a mind is to be a person, and vice versa. Such an equation, when pushed further, would mean that the absence or loss of normal consciousness would involve the absence or loss of personal status. Then unborn children, as well as adults who are asleep or in a coma, would not enjoy the status, dignity and rights of persons.

All in all, medieval and modern themes about persons as inter-related, 'minded', free and supremely valuable beings move beyond the conceptuality of Chalcedon. Nevertheless, the objection that those who still follow Chalcedon in declaring Christ to be 'one person' have kept the word without noticing that it has simply changed its meaning is not on target. Despite the many centuries of development which the term has undergone, there are still some common elements between the use of 'person' in the fifth century and the twenty-first century: as a rational individual that is the centre of action and attribution and in relationship (in Christ's case, to the Father and the Spirit). This justifies retaining, albeit cautiously, the Chalcedonian formula of 'one person in two natures'. I say 'cautiously', since we may well need to challenge some of the ways in which 'person' is understood and used in the modern world: for instance, as a mind or as a conscious, autonomous self, who aims to live a self-sufficient (or should we say simply 'selfish'?) existence. Modern notions of being a person invite scrutiny and may not be automatically accepted without further ado. Some may prefer to speak of Christ as one 'subject' or 'individual'. The drawback here, however, is that personal language is the best and highest language we have. There is a sense of dignity and value automatically involved when we name Christ as one person which may be lacking with the language of 'subject' or 'individual'. The latter language can even be compatible with treating people as 'non-persons' – something which happened to Christ in his passion and death but which his dedicated followers could never bear to happen to him or to any other person.

Personal continuity

One question which did not agitate fifth-century Christians was that of personal continuity. What keeps someone the same person? If Christ is one and the same person in two natures at his conception and birth, how do we account for his remaining continuously this identical person through life and beyond?

We might point to the particular, distinctive assemblage of traits and habits that made up his personal characteristics or recognizable character. At least from a certain point in his childhood, people could begin recognizing his individual traits and habits which made him the uniquely striking 'personality' that he was. But as such Jesus' public character seems more a matter of other people perceiving his personal identity and continuity rather than this continuous personal identity in itself.

Some have tried accounting for personal continuity by pointing to memories. Unquestionably memories have a role in maintaining our sense of personal identity. The memory of what I have personally experienced constitutes the 'evidence' within me (*ad intra*) of my persisting identity. Yet one's enduring personhood cannot simply depend upon one's memory. Otherwise loss of memory would entail loss of personhood. The case of amnesia rebuts any attempts to promote memory as the (sole?) means for constituting and preserving personal continuity or the one life story which is uniquely 'me'. Nevertheless, the sense of continuity provided by memory obviously feeds into and affects our sense of personal identity and our sense of being connected with the past, present and future.

In the case of Christ there is no reason to doubt that the sense of his personal identity mediated through his human mind was shaped in part by his memory. But his memory did not constitute and maintain his personal identity. That must be said firmly, whenever one scents the temptation, which Chapter 2 confronted, to found his eternal, personal pre-existence on a memory of that pre-existence. Christ's human memory began to take shape only with his conception and birth (around 5 BC). Through that memory he could not recall the eternal pre-existence of his own person. We should likewise resist any attempts to account for Christ's personal continuity in his risen and glorious post-existence by appealing to the memories of his earthly existence. Chapter 3 above showed the fragility of such appeals.

In any case, public personality and the connection of memories obviously fail to account for personal continuity in the case of the other two persons of the Trinity. As they were not incarnated, they do not have any directly visible set of public characteristics that might serve to explain their personal continuity. Furthermore, it is only by indulging anthropomorphism that we can speak of the Father and the Holy Spirit 'remembering'; they simply know. Problems about the first and third divine person arise when we bring up another basis for personal continuity, bodily identity and bodily continuity. As they have not been incarnated, bodily continuity cannot bear on their personal continuity. In the case of the incarnate Word of God, however, some kind of bodily persistence seems to bear on the question of the permanent continuity of his person, at least from the time of the incarnation.

Through his body the incarnate Son of God made his human history, that embodied history which was uniquely his. The body that he drew from Mary made possible, not least, the history of ministry which culminated in his passion, death and resurrection from the dead. Through life and beyond death, Christ was and is the same body, albeit now gloriously transformed by his resurrection. He was/is and could/can be recognized as the same person inasmuch as he remains the same body. Bodily identity somehow makes possible personal continuity and identity – at least after the incarnation.

Interchange of properties

Although hardly concerned with the personal continuity of the incarnate Son of God, Christian writers, even centuries before the Council of Chalcedon, practised and reflected on something the union of divinity and humanity in Christ's one person made possible: the 'exchange of properties' or *communicatio idiomatum*. In the run-up to Chalcedon, this exchange of properties emerged as a crucial issue between Cyril of Alexandria (d. 444) and Nestorius, the Patriarch of Constantinople (d. after 451).

Sometimes still defined inaccurately, this exchange means that the attributes of one of his natures can be predicated of Christ even when he is named with reference to his other nature: for example, 'the Son of God died on the cross' or 'the Son of Mary created the world' (see DH 251; ND 605). This method of attribution calls for certain distinctions, so as not to give the impression of confusing the two natures or of attributing directly to one nature what belongs to the other. Thus the Son of God precisely as divine did not die on the cross, nor did the Son of Mary precisely as human create the universe. Nevertheless, because the two natures are united in one personal subject, we can and should maintain the 'exchange of properties'.

Practised by Tertullian and other ancient writers when they spoke of '(the Son of) God being crucified', this exchange of properties often focused on the birth and death of Christ. Hence it often introduced the Virgin Mary who gave birth to the Son of God. Martin Luther (1483–1546) gave voice to a long tradition when he endorsed the exchange of properties in terms not only of Christ's death but also of his human origin from Mary: 'God has suffered; a man created heaven and earth; a man died; God who is from all eternity died; the boy who nurses at the breast of the Virgin Mary is the creator of all things.'[3]

Notes

1. See what was reported from J. Hick in Chapter 1 above.
2. On the development of the notion of 'person' and for an initial bibliography, see H. S. Pyper, 'Person', in *The Oxford Companion to Christian Thought*, 532–3.
3. Cited by P. Althaus, *The Theology of Martin Luther* (Philadelphia: Fortress Press, 1966), 194.

7

Two Minds and Two Wills

Immediately aware that power had gone forth from him, Jesus turned about in the crowd and said, 'Who touched my clothes?' (Mark 5.30)

Abba, Father, for you all things are possible; remove this cup from me. Yet not my will but your will be done. (Mark 14.36)

Through the incarnation the Son of God acquired the mental and volitional life of a human being. In that sense the incarnation brought a 'gain' in his mental and volitional powers. The Son was now capable of human thoughts, as well as of human desires, moral inclinations and freely chosen purposes. He could now acquire knowledge and beliefs by a new route – through human ways of experiencing, thinking, deciding and acting.

Yet the Son's human mind did not and does not enjoy such an independence as to constitute a second person. Many people nowadays, as we saw in the last chapter, can be troubled by the notion of one (divine) person with two minds and two consciousnesses. Surely the presence of two minds compromises Christ's unity as a single person and points to the presence of two persons? But surrendering to that conclusion serves no good purpose. We would finish up, as we also saw in the last chapter, with the divine Word not truly incarnated to become one of us but merely acting in very close tandem with a human agent. If we set our faces against such a conclusion, what might we say about the minds and wills of the incarnate Son of God?

Constantinople III

The Third Council of Constantinople (AD 680/81) followed through on the doctrine of Chalcedon about Christ's two natures. It taught the presence in Christ of two wills (divine and human) and two 'energies' or ways of acting (divine and human). In the face of those heterodox Christians, the so-called Monothelites, who failed to maintain a clear distinction between the human and divine wills of Christ, this Council insisted that the two wills, while never separate and always operating together in perfect harmony, remained nevertheless distinct (DH 556–8; ND 635–7).

What this Council taught about Christ's two wills applies also at the level of his knowledge. Two unseparated but distinct natures also entail two minds: the eternal, divine mind shared in common by the three divine persons, and the human mind acquired by God the Son at the incarnation. Let us take up questions about the two minds and then about the two wills, and try to do so with reverent restraint. It can be hard to be very clear about the workings of our own minds and wills. All the more do we need cautious and awed deference when we reflect on the inner life on a uniquely holy person, one of divine identity who lived 2,000 years ago and about whom the Gospels, or at least those according to Matthew, Mark and Luke, report mainly public actions and words.

The two minds

Some modern scholars, when writing about Christ's two minds, seem to overlook or at least underrate the fact that these two minds exist at infinitely different levels. The divine mind is uncreated and eternal, whereas his human mind was created at a certain point in time. What Thomas Aquinas wrote about Christ's two natures, 'the divine nature exceeds the human by infinity' (*Summa contra Gentiles*, 5.35.8), applies just as much to Christ's two minds. Can we be helped then by analogies between his two consciousnesses (divine and human) and psychological reports of 'divided minds' and multiple personality disorders? In these cases we deal with created minds and personalities, which, whatever painful problems they suffer from, exist essentially at the same level: that of created reality. These cases cannot be expected to illuminate the relationship between Christ's divine and human minds, not only because the cases concern disorders and sometimes pathological disorders, but even more because there remains an infinite qualitative difference between the uncreated and the created mind of the incarnate Word.

With the incarnation the Word of God began to know through two different cognitive systems, a divine and a human way of knowing. If we use this language of two cognitive systems, we need to remember that the two systems are radically unsymmetrical both in their powers and in their results. They are not two different species of one, roughly homogeneous way of knowing, with the first (the human system) yielding much less information than the second (the divine system). The difference between the two systems is not of degree but of kind, the infinite qualitative difference between a created and an uncreated cognitive 'system'. The human system must gather knowledge, gradually and sometimes painfully. The divine system simply knows all things directly and eternally. Second, the human system is sometimes, so to speak, 'switched off' – for example, when we fall asleep or are knocked unconscious. But the divine system of knowing can never be switched off or on; the divine mind is always 'on' and is never asleep. Third, at least during the earthly life of Jesus, the person of the Word (through his divine mind) knew fully and possessed completely the human mind of Jesus as his own human mind, but not vice versa. The divine mind and consciousness had access to and 'included' the human mind and consciousness, but not vice versa.

For centuries Catholic teachers followed the doctrine of Thomas Aquinas about the human mind of the incarnate Son of God, who, even from the very first moment of his conception, possessed the face-to-face beatific vision of God which the blessed enjoy in heaven. Thus Jesus lived his earthly life 'by sight', and not by faith. Notable difficulties can be brought against the thesis that Jesus' human knowledge embraced the beatific vision.

First, how could he have genuinely suffered if through his human mind he knew God immediately and in a beatifying way? Second, such a vision raises problems for the free operation of Jesus' human will. Despite the way Aquinas qualifies somewhat Jesus' knowledge by vision (ST 3a.3.10.ad 2), such an immediate, beatifying vision of God in this life, because it involves total knowledge, would seem to rule out the possibility of human freedom under the conditions of earthly history. Here and now the exercise of freedom requires some limits in our knowledge and some uncertainties about the future. Third, Jesus was remembered to have remained obedient towards his Father, despite trials and temptations (e.g. Mark 1.12–13; 14.32–42; Luke 22.8; Hebrews 2.18; 4.15). The steady possession of the beatific vision would seem to rule out any genuine struggle on the part of Jesus. His trials and temptations would not have been real threats to his loyalty but only a show put on for our benefit and edification. Fourth, how can one reconcile the knowledge of vision (which

Aquinas interprets as also including a comprehensive grasp of all creatures and everything they could do) with Jesus' human knowledge of the world? Precisely as human, such knowledge grows and develops through experience, but always remains limited. A knowledge in this life which entailed (right from conception itself) a comprehensive grasp of all creatures and everything they could do appears to be so superhuman that it casts serious doubts on the genuine status of Jesus' human knowledge.

Fifth, the thesis of such a comprehensive knowledge right from the moment of conception has its own special difficulties. The mind is certainly not to be reduced to the brain. Nevertheless, the mind correlates 1:1 with a brain; mental life depends on a brain. What could we make of Jesus' human brain at the single-cell stage being associated with and in some sense 'supporting' the most 'advanced' human knowledge imaginable, the beatific vision enjoyed by saints in heaven after they have completed their earthly pilgrimage? According to a classical adage, 'grace builds on nature'. Here we would have an extraordinarily high grace, the very vision of God enjoyed by those in glory, building on the utterly simple point of departure for the growth of his human nature, Jesus at the single-cell stage.

Sixth, the Gospels of Matthew, Mark and Luke, along with some indications of special knowledge, also contain passages that suggest ordinary limits in Jesus' human knowledge (e.g. Mark 5.30–2; 6.6). Some early Christian writers tried to blunt the force of such admissions as 'no one knows the day or the hour [of the end of the age], neither the angels in heaven, nor the Son, but only the Father' (Mark 13.32). Thus Augustine explained that Jesus did know but was not prepared to announce the hour (*De Trinitate*, 1.23). But other ancient writers recognized that the Gospels report limits to Jesus' human knowledge. Even such an unchallengeable champion of Jesus' divinity as St Cyril of Alexandria (d. 444) took Luke at his word, when he wrote of Jesus 'increasing in wisdom and in years' (Luke 2.52).

Seventh, the Council of Chalcedon's insistence on Christ's human nature preserving the 'character proper' to it (DH 302; ND 615) should make one cautious about attributing special properties (in this case the quite extraordinary knowledge of the beatific vision) to his human mind. Christ's human mind and knowledge were maintained and not made superhuman by the hypostatic union. A comprehensive grasp of *all* creatures and *all* they can do (which Aquinas attributes to the beatific vision) would lift Christ's knowledge so clearly beyond the normal limits of human knowledge as to cast serious doubts on the genuineness of his humanity, at least in one essential aspect. It would picture him during his earthly history as being in his human mind for all intents and purposes omniscient, even if not necessarily omniscient as God is in the divine mind.

For these and related reasons it is hard to maintain Aquinas' thesis that the earthly Jesus' knowledge included (surely one would have to say was dominated by?) the beatific vision. Here, at least for Roman Catholics who still hanker after Aquinas' thesis which held sway till the mid-twentieth century, it is advisable to notice that several documents from the International Theological Commission (1979, 1981 and 1983) and from the Pontifical Biblical Commission (1984) dealt with Jesus' human consciousness and knowledge but never claimed that he enjoyed the beatific vision during his earthly life. Likewise the *Catechism of the Catholic Church* (1992) never attributed this vision to the human mind of Jesus during his life on earth. Such texts from the late twentieth century reflect the way in which Aquinas' 'maximal' view of the earthly Jesus' knowledge no longer enjoys official endorsement, even if some individuals continue to defend it.

The two wills

Some sayings of Christ that differentiated between his will and that of his Father proved critical in debates that preceded Constantinople III and its teaching on Christ's human and divine wills. In Gethsemane Jesus prayed: 'Abba, Father, for you all things are possible; remove this cup from me; yet, not what I want, but what you want' (Mark 14.36). Mainstream Christians, when interpreting this passage or its equivalents in the other Gospels, normally commented: 'Not what I as man will, but what you and I as God will.' Since Christ through his human will desired not to die, we might speak of a non-sinful 'discord' or tension between his human will and the divine will he shared with the Father. Constantinople III, when distinguishing between Christ's human and divine wills, insisted, however, that they functioned together in perfect harmony, as happened in what ensued at Gethsemane. This conciliar teaching followed from the NT's repeated insistence that Jesus as a matter of fact (*de facto*) lived a sinless life of perfect obedience to his Father's will (e.g. Hebrews 4.15; 5.8; John 8.46).

Christ's sinlessness *de facto* almost inevitably raised a question *de iure*: in principle could he have sinned? Was he immune from sin, that is to say, intrinsically impeccable? Those who hold this position have to face a range of challenging questions: how, for instance, could such *de iure* impeccability be reconciled with Jesus' being tempted and tested as the NT recalls (e.g. Mark 1.13; Hebrews 4.15)? If he truly felt tempted – and that must mean feeling tempted inwardly – how could this be coherent with the claim that he was intrinsically impeccable? Here, after having taken my distance from Thomas Aquinas' exaggerated claim about the unique level of the earthly Jesus' human knowledge, on the question of Jesus' sinlessness, do I now turn around and join with Aquinas in maintaining that it was impossible for

Christ to sin (ST 3.18.4)? Yet I think that such sinlessness *de iure* should be held.

First of all, the Gospels of Mark, Matthew and Luke portray Jesus as having an overwhelming sense of the presence of God and an unreserved openness to the love of God. Jesus was totally given to the service of the divine kingdom. Since that was so, all temptations were bound to fail. Second, these Gospels and, in particular, that of Luke tell us of the Holy Spirit anointing Jesus for his role as Redeemer. The Spirit sanctified and elevated the human being of Jesus to be worthy of a union with the eternal Son of God. Jesus exercised his human freedom through the Holy Spirit. To admit even the possibility of sin would brand this work of the Spirit as somehow deficient.

One can pile up arguments like this in support of Jesus' *de iure* sinlessness, as I did in *Christology: a Biblical, Historical, and Systematic Study of Jesus*.[1] Ultimately, the arguments reduce to one: the status of Jesus' moral goodness and impeccability is not to be examined simply and solely in terms of his human nature. We sin or refrain from sinning as persons. After falling into sin, one could not convincingly excuse oneself by saying: 'It wasn't me but only my human nature that sinned.' The question under discussion should be phrased: was Christ personally impeccable *de iure*? The answer must be yes. Otherwise we would face the situation of God possibly in deliberate opposition to God; one divine person would be capable (through his human will) of committing sin and so intentionally transgressing the divine will. The possibility of Christ sinning seems incompatible with the divine identity of his person.

It is in these terms that I must respond to the criticism levelled against me by the late William Dych on the issue of Jesus' *de iure* sinlessness. My 'real reason' for recognizing in Jesus an inability to sin does not lie in any need 'to balance and juggle the competing claims' of his two natures, but in the personal identity of Jesus.[2] It is the divine status of his person that rules out the possibility of sin. God cannot sin against God.

Christ's personal identity, rather than anything that made him less human than other members of Adam's race, changed his *manner* of being human and living as a human being. In his earthly existence Christ set before us a *new* manner of impeccable, utterly holy living, which anticipated the final sinlessness and lasting holiness to which we are all called and which will be revealed at the goal of our redemption.

This chapter has tackled issues about the two minds and two wills that are the necessary corollary of Christ's two natures recognized by the Council of Chalcedon. Granted the duality of his humanity and divinity, what about their union? This will be the theme of the next chapter.

Notes

1. Oxford: Oxford University Press, 1995, 268–71.
2. W. V. Dych, *Thy Kingdom Come: Jesus and the Reign of God* (New York: Crossroad, 1999), 50.

The Mode of Union

Just as a rational soul and a body form a single human person, so God and man form one Christ. (The Athanasian Creed)

How should we envisage the union expressed by the classical term for the incarnation: the hypostatic union? It stands for the union existing between a divine person or *hypostasis*, the Word of God with his divine nature (shared eternally with the Father and the Holy Spirit) and the human nature he acquires at the incarnation. What might we say positively, or at least what might we exclude when talking about the hypostatic union? How do Christ's divinity and humanity exist and work together to form a single, historical individual?

The Old Testament

The OT offers a variety of ways in which God can be causally related to what is not God. The timeless (eternal), all-spiritual God has relations with temporal and material things and persons: for instance, by creating and conserving them or by acting in special ways towards them. The range of possibilities is generous: God can be united with persons and with non-personal realities. Thus God 'appears' to Moses at the burning bush and repeatedly 'speaks through' the prophets. Stories about the patriarchs tell of God in human appearance 'wrestling' with Jacob (Genesis 32.22–32), 'speaking' to Jacob (Genesis 35.1), 'hearing' the cries of Hagar's child, Ishmael (Genesis 21.14–21), 'calling' Abraham and Sarah to leave their country (Genesis 12.1–3), and 'putting to the test' Abraham (Genesis 22.1–19). The story of Israel witnesses to the lasting results of such divine actions. But in themselves such special actions remain transitory: any appearing, speaking, wrestling, calling or testing is quickly over. In the case of God 'taking possession' of a piece of ground, being 'enthroned on Zion', or 'dwelling in' Zion (e.g. Psalms 84.1; 132.12–14; Ezekiel 10.3–4; 43.1–4), we are meant to think of something more permanent, a relationship or union that will last. But such cases relate a personal God to impersonal, created realities. Nowhere does the OT talk of God permanently taking possession, for instance, of a priest, a prophetess or a king.

However, a certain permanence emerges in the language of the glory of God 'returning to', 'filling' and 'residing in' the Temple (e.g. Ezekiel 10.3–4; 43.1–4). This abiding presence of the glorious God, which was a source of grace for pilgrims to and residents of the Temple, prepared the way for belief in the personal presence of the Son of God in Jesus. The incarnation offered the supremely intense form of divine presence. In the fourth century AD, St Athanasius was to use this 'dwelling-in-the-Temple' language and wrote of the invisible God dwelling in the visible temple of Christ's humanity (*De Incarnatione Verbi*, 8).

The OT, in short, yields some help for those who want to reflect on a unique causal relationship beween God and the created humanity of Christ. In particular, the divine glory in the Temple foreshadows the union entailed in the Word of God being enfleshed or incarnated in a visible, human being.

A mingling?

The issue of the union of divinity and humanity in the incarnate Word became critical from the late fourth century. Back in 325 the First Council of Nicaea had defended Christ's true divinity against Arius (d. 336) and his followers. Intent on protecting the Nicene faith in Christ's divinity, Apollinarius of Laodicea (d. *c.* 390) underinterpreted the humanity of Christ, and argued that in the incarnation the Word assumed a living body but took the place of the spiritual, rational soul. Apollinarius was an easy target for St Gregory of Nazianzus (d. *c.* 389) and St Gregory of Nyssa (d. *c.* 395). The former gave the classical formulation to the principle that to have healed and saved us, Christ must also be truly and fully human: 'the unassumed is the unhealed' (*Epistola,* 101.32). If the incarnation entailed assuming only a living, human body, our rational souls would have remained 'unhealed' and unredeemed. Gregory of Nazianzus, as a leading figure at the First Council of Constantinople in 381, collaborated in condemning Apollinarian reduction of Christ's integral humanity (DH 151; ND 13).

In upholding Christ's true divinity against Arians and perfect humanity against the Apollinarians, how were mainstream Christians to conceive the unity in Christ? Decades were to pass before it became clear that the union should be seen as taking place in his one person and not in his two natures. The one *person* is the principle of unity, the *natures* constitute Christ's duality – to use the language of Chalcedon. Before that Council met in 451, some false paths had been followed.

The two Gregorys, although they contributed to the development of teaching and terminology about Christ, also exemplify the problem created by presuming that Christ's unity is to be explored at the level of his natures. They presented his unity by using Stoic language about the 'mixing' and 'blending' of the two natural substances which completely permeate each other without losing their characteristic nature. The obvious problem with this doctrine of mixture is that it makes Christ out to be a kind of amalgam, a divine–human hybrid, as well as moving too much in the area of material categories. It would take time to move beyond such attempts to interpret Christ's unity in terms of his two natures, no matter whether this nature–nature relationship was explained through categories of 'mingling' or in other ways.

It is not that the two Gregorys began the habit of explaining as 'mingling' the union of divinity and humanity in Christ. Back in the second century, St Irenaeus (d. *c.* 200) wrote of Christ's 'advent in the flesh' as effecting 'the mingling and uniting of God and man' (*Adversus haereses*, 4.20.4). A few years later, when arguing for a genuine incarnation against Marcion, Tertullian (d. *c.* 225) wrote of the Son 'mingling in himself man and God' (*Adversus Marcionem*, 2.27). Yet the same Tertullian also insisted that the union of humanity and divinity in the one person of Christ did not entail a 'mixture' (*Adversus Praxean*, 27.8–9). In the fifth century St Cyril of Alexandria (d. 444), despite his strong emphasis on the unity of Christ, explicitly rejected the terminology of mingling as a way of accounting for the incarnation (*Quod unus sit Christus*, 737a–b). A few years later Eutyches, a one-sided and unsophisticated follower of Cyril, paid the price for the ambiguous inadequacy of the 'mingling/blending' language. He apparently argued that after the union effected by the incarnation Christ's human nature is simply absorbed by the divine nature, as a drop of honey can be swallowed up by an immense sea. In its 451 definition the Council of Chalcedon insisted that the one person of Christ has been revealed in two natures, without their being 'blended or changed'.

Body/soul analogy

Despite (or because of?) its innumerable occurrences, the mysterious and remarkably close union between the soul and body of human beings invited Christians to seek there an analogy to the unique, once-and-for-all union of divinity and humanity in the person of the incarnate Son of God. This analogy turns up in a letter by St Augustine of Hippo: 'just as in any man (except for that one who was uniquely assumed) soul and body form one person, so in Christ, the Word and the Man form one person' (*Epistola*, 169.2.8). A few years later St Cyril of Alexandria used the same comparison in his third letter written (in Greek) to (or should one say against?) Nestorius (AD 430). Apparently composed around the same time and in Latin, the so-called Athanasian Creed endorsed this analogy: 'just as a rational soul and a body form a single human person, so God and man are one Christ'. In the next century Severus of Antioch (d. 538) compared the union between the two natures of the incarnate Word to the wedding of the soul and body in a human individual.

The analogy enjoys some positive features. As with the union between Christ's humanity and divinity, so the union between soul and body is remarkably close and mysterious. It also involves spiritual and material components and unequal 'partners' (soul/body; divinity/humanity). The major difficulty with this analogy, however, is that, in the case of body (matter) and soul (form), we are dealing with incomplete natures or substances that together make up one complete substance (a human being). In the case of the incarnate Son of God, two complete substances – his perfect human nature and perfect divinity – are united. Any analogy of the hyposta-tic union with the union of body and soul fails to be very illuminating. The union of body and soul may be uniquely 'tight', but the two components have a different, lesser status than the two involved in the hypostatic union. Second, death

will separate them – at least for some time or stage. Third,
this analogy means using the union (of body and soul) within
one 'part' of the incarnate Son of God, namely his humanity
or human 'part', to illuminate the union of that 'part' with the
divine 'part' (his divinity) of the 'whole' which forms the
incarnate Son of God. That can seem a cumbersome,
awkward procedure.

Not surprisingly, an analogy similar to the 'wedding' of
body and soul turned up in Christian writings down to the
mid-fifth century. The imagery used in the Song of Songs to
celebrate the union between the bridegroom and the bride
was sometimes pressed into service to illuminate the meeting
of the divine and the human in the incarnation. The divine
Word who became flesh embraced within himself humanity.
Thus the human soul of Christ was taken to be the bridal
partner in the loving grasp of the incarnate Word.[1]

After the time of Chalcedon the imagery of the bridegroom
and the bride came to be applied to the loving relationship
between Christ and the Church or between Christ and the
individual believer. This imagery, which deals with the union
of love between two distinct persons, did not and does not
work properly in the case of the incarnation. There the
divinity and humanity of the Word made flesh do not as such
constitute two distinct persons but rather two distinct
natures. Besides, they are radically dissimilar – something
that does not hold true of the bridegroom and bride.

Nevertheless, it is not surprising that these two similar
analogies, that of the body and soul and that of the bridegroom and bride, were tried out on the incarnation. After all,
the challenging closeness of these two unions has repeatedly
caught the attention of thinkers and writers. Even if death
inevitably separates body and soul, and even if lovers, despite
their hunger for eternal union, can be separated, the compact
partnership of these two cases readily suggested comparison
with the hypostatic union. However, the analogies do not take

us very far when reflecting on Christ's union of divinity and humanity, since the first union (that of body and soul) concerns two incomplete substances or natures, whereas the second (between bridegroom and bride) concerns two distinct persons. The incarnation, however, is constituted by one and only one person in two complete and perfect natures. Add too the fact that the incarnation entails an eternal, inseparable union between humanity and divinity, whereas the union of body and soul inevitably breaks down (at death) and the union between lovers frequently does so.

Scripture, the Church and the Trinity

The union of body with soul and of bridegroom with bride, the first an analogy drawn from within one person and the second drawn from a relationship between two persons, may be stunning comparisons, but have nothing particularly Christian about them. They are analogies coming from universal human experience. Three other analogies, which have been applied to the union of divinity and humanity in the incarnate Son of God, belong rather to what we know through divine revelation and human faith. The first two have been invoked to illuminate, not so much the incarnation itself, but rather the union of the human and the divine in the composition of the Scriptures and in the make-up of the Church, respectively.

Drawing on St John Chrysostom (d. 407), the Second Vatican Council in its 1965 Constitution on Divine Revelation (*Dei Verbum*) drew a parallel between the two natures of the incarnate Christ and the two essential properties of the inspired Scriptures as the Word of God expressed in the words of men (no. 13). Nearly 30 years later the Pontifical Biblical Commission also remarked on the divine and human characteristics of the Scriptures. That document appealed to the 'truth of the incarnation' and stated: 'the inspired Word of

God has been expressed in human language, and . . . this Word has been expressed, under divine inspiration, by human authors possessed of limited capacities and resources'.[2]

This analogy with the incarnation functions well. Just as the incarnate Son of God is truly divine and fully human, so the Scriptures result inseparably from the work of God and from the human work of the sacred authors. An intriguing addition to the analogy can be spotted in the Biblical Commission's insistence that the human authors of the Scriptures possessed and deployed 'limited capacities and resources'. The human nature assumed at the incarnation by the Son of God was and remains similarly limited. To allege that Christ's humanity in itself enjoyed and enjoys unlimited or infinite capacities and resources would be to cast fatal doubt on its genuinely human status.

As regards the Church, Pope Pius XII in his encyclical 'The Mystical Body of Jesus Christ' endorsed an analogy between (a) the visible humanity of Christ and his invisible divinity, and (b) the visible and invisible properties of 'the Mystical Body', the Church.[3] In its 1964 Dogmatic Constitution on the Church (*Lumen Gentium*), the Second Vatican Council, albeit more cautiously, presented the Church as a mysterious spiritual reality appearing as a visible organization – somewhat in the same way that Christ's human presence both manifests and cloaks his inseparable divinity. In both cases we encounter 'one complex reality made up of a human and a divine element: just as the nature, which he has assumed and which is inseparably united to him, serves the divine Word as a living instrument of salvation, so, in a somewhat similar way, does the social structure of the Church serve the Spirit of Christ who vivifies it' (*Lumen Gentium*, 8).

In the case of these two analogies we find Pius XII, Vatican II and the Biblical Commission practising a method recommended by the First Vatican Council (1869/70): namely, that of seeking further insights by comparing revealed truths with one another (DH 3016; ND 132). Obviously such comparing and contrasting can help to deepen one's understanding and appreciation of the truths in question. Appropriate analogies do not function by proving something or by adding to our knowledge and beliefs things which we did not previously know. Instead, by invoking and relating things we already know and/or believe, appropriate analogies yield fresh insights, but without denying what is dissimilar and different.

The two analogies just recalled remind believers that, just as they distinguish without separating the divine and human natures of Christ, so they should distinguish without separating (a) the divine Author and the visible, human authors of the Bible and (b) the divine Spirit of Christ and the public community of the Church. In both cases we meet a 'complex' reality made up of divine and human elements. At the same time, differences come through. Christ's divine and human natures are united in his one person, whereas many human authors collaborated in producing the various texts which make up one Bible. Likewise, while confessing the Church to be 'one' and forming one 'mystical' body or person, baptized Christians are innumerably many. Furthermore, the sacred writers, the Holy Spirit who inspires them, the members of the Church, and the Spirit of Christ are all complete persons, whereas the divine and human natures of Christ do not precisely as such constitute one person. Quite the opposite. The person of the Son of God establishes the union between his divine and his human nature by assuming the latter. Nevertheless, provided we recognize these various differences, the two analogies enjoy a certain value.

A third analogy, taken from the notion of the 'perichoresis' or reciprocal presence and interpenetration of the three persons of the Trinity, proves less helpful and looks open to serious misunderstandings. Emerging in the fourth century and more fully worked out by St John Damascene (d. *c.* 749), the idea of perichoresis ('going around') illuminates a little the most intimate and infinitely loving inter-relationship between God the Father, God the Son and God the Holy Spirit. Some authors have applied the language of perichoresis and 'interpenetration' to the divinity and humanity of Christ. The problem here is not simply that trinitarian perichoresis concerns the relationship between three persons, whereas perichoresis applied to Christ bears on the relationship between two natures. The deeper challenge goes back to the Council of Chalcedon. How can we talk of the interpenetration of Christ's two natures without lapsing into the error of imagining them to be mingled or 'confused'?[4] Such an analogy taken from the inner life of the Trinity to illuminate the union between Christ's divinity and humanity seems misleading rather than enlightening.

After spending a number of chapters reflecting on what the incarnation meant, let us now turn to examine how it took place historically: through the virginal conception.

Notes

1. See M. W. Elliott, *The Song of Songs and Christology in the Early Church 381–451* (Tübingen: Mohr Siebeck, 2000).
2. 'The Interpretation of the Bible in the Church', *Origins* 23 (6 January 1994), 497–524, at 500 and 510.
3. *Acta Apostolicae Sedis* 35 (1943), 223–4.
4. What was said above (Chapter 5) about Christ's 'mixed' actions that involved the simultaneous operation of his divine and human powers was not meant to suggest any 'mingling' or perichoretic confusing of such powers.

9

The Virginal Conception

All this took place to fulfil what had been spoken by the
Lord through the prophet. 'Look, the virgin shall
conceive and bear a son . . .' (Matthew 1.22–3)

> Was this His coming! I had hoped to see
> A scene of wondrous glory, as was told
> Of some great God who in a rain of gold
> Broke open bars and fell on Danaë.
> (Oscar Wilde, 'Ave Maria Gratia Plena')

In what way did the incarnation happen historically? Mainstream Christianity has followed the Gospels of Matthew and
Luke in pointing to the virginal conception or Mary's conceiving Jesus through the power of the Holy Spirit and without
the co-operation of a human father. Thus this belief main-
tains that Christ's incarnation did not follow the ordinary
laws of procreation but was the fruit of a special action by the
Holy Spirit. For the sake of clarity it is important to insist
that we reflect here on the way Christ was *conceived* and not
on the way he was born. In other words, we speak of his
virginal conception and not, as many inaccurately do, of his
'virgin birth'.

The virginal conception and the incarnation

Christian thinkers have regularly acknowledged that the incarnation did not have to happen through a virginal conception. Such a conception does not appear to be strictly essential to the event of the incarnation. In principle, the Son of God could have assumed a human nature in some other way – above all, through the normal conditions of human generation. But in fact this was not the way it happened. As we shall see later in this chapter, the event of the virginal conception introduced and illuminated wonderfully what was to follow in the whole story of Jesus. Like many other features in the history of Jesus, events could have followed a different course. He might, for instance, have been stoned to death like St Stephen or beheaded like St John the Baptist. But in fact he died by crucifixion, and from the start of Christianity believers felt called to contemplate and scrutinize the meaning of Jesus' actual death. What happened at the start of his human story (the virginal conception) and at the end (the crucifixion) invites our reverential reflection. We do better to ponder what actually happened rather than indulge alternate scenarios and think about what might have happened.

Another initial comment concerns Islam. The Koran accepts the virginal conception of Jesus as an historical event. Yet Muslims do not recognize him as the incarnate Son of God; their strict monopersonal faith in God excludes believing Jesus to be anything more than a remarkable prophet. What interests me here is that the official teaching of over 1,000 million people says yes to the virginal conception but no to any incarnation. Conversely we have some Christians saying yes to the incarnation but no to any virginal conception.[1] Wolfhart Pannenberg (b. 1928), for instance, uncharacteristically lapses into extreme language when he declares: 'in its content, the legend [!] of the Jesus' virgin birth [Pannenberg means conception] stands in an irreconcilable contradiction to the Christology of the incarnation of the preexistent Son of God found in Paul and John'. A few pages later Pannenberg again insists that the concepts of virginal conception and pre-existence 'cannot be connected without contradiction'.[2] There may be some conceptual argument lurking in the neighbourhood, but it eludes me. All this looks rather like gratuitous assertion. When a pre-existent, divine person acquires a human nature, why could this not happen through a virginal conception? Why on earth must talk of virginal conception, which concerns the historical origins of Christ's *human nature*, rule out the eternal pre-existence of his *person* and vice versa?

Naturally impossible?

Belief in the virginal conception comes under fire from various quarters and for various reasons. Some dismiss it as scientifically impossible or simply ruled out by the laws of nature. In any case, if by some freakish chance Mary conceived a child by parthenogenesis, or reproduction from an ovum without fertilization by a sperm, the offspring would have been a female baby. Left to 'their own resources', women do not have the Y chromosome necessary to produce a male child.

Everyone negotiates this kind of argument in terms of their notion of God. Those who accept that God has created the world along with the natural laws which govern its working should have no trouble in also accepting that, for good reasons, God could and will in special cases override the normal working of these laws. In doing so, God is not, as some continue to say, 'violating' such laws. On the occasion of the incarnation, a once-and-for-all assuming of the human condition by the divine Word, God might be expected to do something unique in bringing it about. Those who stress the

'natural' impossibility of the virginal conception might well
be asked to re-examine their picture of God.

An historical borrowing?

Some writers claim that early Christians fashioned the
virginal conception stories (picked up later by Matthew and
Luke) by borrowing from Greco-Roman legends of extraordinary births of mythical or actual heroes. Since they
acknowledged Jesus' divine origin and status, Christians of
the first century took over and applied to him current legends
about the conception and birth of such heroes as Herakles,
Romulus and Remus, Plato, Alexander the Great and
Augustus Caesar.

In 'Ave Maria Gratia Plena' Oscar Wilde (1854–1900)
provides the short answer to this theory. The story of the
Annunciation (Luke 1.26–38) differs strikingly from the
myth of Zeus entering through a narrow hole and in a shower
of gold to impregnate Danaë, and from the myth of Zeus
coming to Semele in his true shape. His thunderbolts slew
her but rendered her son (Dionysus) immortal. Zeus put the
unborn child in his thigh, and from there he was born at the
due time. Zeus' lustful desire for Danaë and Semele's hunger
for Zeus struck Wilde as utterly different from the 'supreme
mystery of Love' found in the story of the angelic annunciation to Mary and Jesus' conception:

> Was this His coming! I had hoped to see
> A scene of wondrous glory, as was told
> Of some great God who in a rain of gold
> Broke open bars and fell on Danaë:
> Or a dread vision as when Semele,
> Sickening for love and unappeased desire,
> Prayed to see God's clear body, and the fire
> Caught her brown limbs and slew her utterly.

With such glad dreams I sought this holy place,
And now with wondering eyes and heart I stand
Before this supreme mystery of Love:
Some kneeling girl with passionless pale face,
An angel with a lily in his hand,
And over both the white wings of a Dove.

Wilde expected that the story of Jesus' conception would match myths of the sexual exploits of Zeus and other deities. Wilde found something very different and much more mysterious.

A longer answer to the thesis of borrowed legends comes by examining the alleged parallels. Over and over again one can spot startling differences between these legends and the virginal conception accounts of Matthew and Luke. The Greco-Roman stories tell of sexual intercourse between a deity and a woman who is sometimes tricked into having relations or even raped by the god in question. Unlike the Annunciation story, where Mary's conscious agreement features prominently (Luke 1.26–38), the Greco-Roman legends generally turn such mothers of mythical heroes as Danaë (who begets Perseus) into mere tools of divine passion and projects. The smutty tone of these legends, which often feature mythical figures who (unlike Mary and Jesus) do not belong to human history, can verge on soft pornography. It seems unimaginable that early Christians, coming from a Jewish background and immersed in the Jewish scriptures, could consider such legends useful sources for illuminating the human origins of Jesus. Nowhere do these scriptures attribute to YHWH the sexual activity and trickery ascribed to Zeus and other deities said to have fathered mythical heroes and exceptional human beings. Let us see some examples.

Diodorus Siculus, a first-century BC writer, drew heavily on a second-century source to recount the legend of the conception, birth and subsequent labours of Herakles. Supposedly herself the great-granddaughter of Zeus, Alkmene 'was taken by Zeus, through a deceit, and she gave birth to Herakles'. Thus this hero, according to his mythical family tree, was both the son and the great-great-grandson of Zeus, 'the greatest of the gods'. Diodorus described the deceit of Zeus as follows:

> When Zeus lay with Alkmene, he tripled the length of the night, and, in the increased length of time spent in begetting the child, he foreshadowed the exceptional power of the child who was to be begotten. All in all, this union did not take place because of erotic desire, as with other women, but more for the purpose of creating the child. Because he wished to make the intercourse legitimate and did not wish to take Alkmene by force, nor could he ever hope to seduce her because of her self-control, therefore, Zeus chose deceit. By this means he tricked Alkmene: he became like Amphitryon [her husband] in every way.

Subsequently Zeus' wife, Hera, jealous at what had happened, succeeded in stopping for a time the labour pains of Alkmene. After Herakles was eventually born, Hera even sent 'two snakes to destroy the baby, but the child did not panic. He grabbed the neck of each snake in his two hands and strangled them' (*Universal History*, 4.9.1–10). It is not credible that this legend of Herakles' conception and birth provided a workable model for the accounts of the virginal conception provided by Matthew and Luke.

Livy (d. AD 12 or 17) tells briefly the story of the conception and birth of the legendary founders of Rome, Romulus and Remus. Their mother, Rhea Silvia, had been forced by her wicked uncle, who had usurped the throne of Alba Longa, to become a vestal virgin. Then she 'was violated and gave birth to twins. She named Mars as their father, either because she really believed that, or because the fault might appear less heinous if a deity were the cause of it'. The cruel king threw her into prison and had the babies left in a cradle on the banks of the Tiber. They were suckled by a kindly she-wolf, and grew up to found the city of Rome (*The History of Rome*, 1.4). A Greek writer, Dionysius of Halicarnassus (d. early in the first century AD), gives three versions of how Rhea Silvia was violated in the course of her duties as a vestal virgin. The three versions ascribe the rape to one of her suitors, to her evil uncle (Amulius), or to the god Mars (*Roman Antiquities*, 1.76–7). Once again one would require a wild leap of the historical imagination to think that these stories about Romulus and Remus furnished a source for early Christians bent on creating a 'fitting' account of Jesus' conception and birth.

What of Greco-Roman legends about the origin of such genuinely historical figures as Plato and Alexander the Great? The god of wisdom, Phoebus Apollo, was sometimes credited with providing Amphictione, Plato's mother, with superior, divine sperm for the conception of her brilliant offspring. To bring about the desired effect from this sperm, her human husband was prevented from having sexual intercourse with her.[3]

Even during his lifetime many believed that Alexander the Great's mother, Olympias, had conceived him through intercourse with Zeus. The god appeared in the form of 'a great snake' (a classical penis symbol) and wound himself around her body while Olympias was asleep (Plutarch, 'Alexander', *Parallel Lives*, 2.1–3.2). Suetonius (born c. AD 69), drawing on an earlier Greek source, tells a similar story about the god Apollo assuming the form of a snake and coming in the middle of the night, when she was asleep, to impregnate Atia, the mother of the Emperor Augustus (*Lives of the Caesars*, 2.94.4). These stories of what happened during the night to the sleeping Olympias and Atia stand in striking contrast with Luke's Annunciation story. Mary is fully awake, accepts the divine invitation to collaborate in the incarnation, and does so without any sexual intercourse taking place. Whatever the historical status of the various details in Luke's text, it stands worlds apart from the stories told by Plutarch and Suetonius about Olympias and Atia, respectively.

Let me finish with Joseph Campbell, who dedicates a section of *The Hero with a Thousand Faces* to the 'womb of redemption' (pp. 264–8). He claims that the story of Jesus' virginal conception 'is recounted everywhere' and with 'striking uniformity'. Reading the alleged parallels cited by Campbell, one can only ask: what counts as 'striking uniformity' for him? A story he cites from Colombia tells of a virgin conceiving by the first rays of the rising sun; she brings forth an emerald, which later turns into a male child. Campbell mentions the Buddha descending 'from heaven to his mother's womb in the shape of a milk-white elephant', an Aztec story of a deity 'in the form of a ball of feathers' approaching a woman, and a Tongan tale of a woman giving birth to a clam that in turn produces 'a fine, big baby boy'. Inevitably Campbell also presses into service legends of Zeus assuming the form of a shower of gold, a bull or a swan, so as to impregnate women of his choice.

What has all this to do with Jesus' virginal conception as we find it set out in the opening chapters of Matthew and Luke? The resemblances between the Gospel accounts and Campbell's alleged parallels fail to establish any 'uniformity', let alone 'striking uniformity'. The resemblances are at best slight and superficial: some kind of unusual conception (and birth) which produces a remarkable figure. The contrasts are overwhelming. Where do Matthew and Luke introduce sexual intercourse and anything like the rising sun, white elephants, balls of feathers, clams, bulls, swans or showers of gold? If they ever heard of Greco-Roman legends about Zeus enjoying romantic escapades by assuming the shape of a bull, a swan or a shower of gold, Jewish Christians represented by Matthew's Gospel and Gentile Christians represented by Luke's Gospel would have dismissed such sexual capers as quite loathsome. In the second century St Justin Martyr (d. *c.* 165) considered the promiscuous behaviour attributed to Zeus revolting – worthy of a deity 'overcome by the love of evil and shameful pleasures' (*First Apology*, 21). The victim of a master theory, Campbell deluded himself with his talk of 'striking uniformity'. He could never have made such a claim, if he had taken time to count up the many sharp differences between the parallels he cited and what we read in the Gospels. Oscar Wilde was right in being properly sensitive to these differences.

Biblical texts and Christian narratives

Some commentators have looked to the OT Scriptures when explaining the source of the virginal conception stories in Matthew and Luke. The Gospel writers and/or their sources, far from reporting a unique event brought about by God's special action, developed their narratives of the virginal conception simply and solely by reflecting on the sacred texts they had inherited. At first glance this explanation enjoys more plausibility than attempts to account for the virginal conception as a Christian adaptation of some Greco-Roman legends. After all, the NT authors were clearly steeped in the Jewish scriptures and constantly echoed or quoted these inspired texts. Yet does such a 'scriptural' explanation account satisfactorily for the virginal conception stories?

Ten times in his Gospel, from Chapters 1 to 27, Matthew introduced 'fulfilment' formulas. The first such formula reads: 'All this [the virginal conception] took place to fulfil what had been spoken by the Lord through the prophet: "Look the virgin shall conceive and bear a son, and they shall

name him Emmanuel", which means "God is with us"'
(Matthew 1.22–3). The OT text Matthew had in mind comes
from Isaiah 7.14, which in the original Hebrew announces
the conception of a child, to be born of a 'young woman
(*almah*)'; this sign is best understood as a son who will be
born to the king's wife and who will thus ensure the continu-
ation of the Davidic dynasty through the faithful providence
of God, once again shown to be 'God with us'. The Greek
translation (in the LXX or Septuagint version) renders
almah as *parthenos* or 'virgin', as in the version quoted by
Matthew who, most likely, knew the Hebrew original but
decided to use the Greek translation. Two comments seem
called for here.

First, we do not have any evidence that in pre-NT times
the Greek version of Isaiah 7.14 was 'understood to predict a
virginal conception, since it need mean no more than that the
girl who is now a virgin will ultimately conceive (in a natural
way)'.[4] Second, the first of Matthew's ten fulfilment formulas
should presumably be interpreted in the light of the other
nine. In those subsequent cases Matthew looks for a more or
less appropriate biblical text to illuminate some event he
reports. In other words, he moves from event to text, rather
than creating some 'event' out of the biblical texts. One can
reasonably hold that, after receiving from an oral or written
tradition an account of the virginal conception, Matthew
looks for a suitable text to illuminate the story and finds such
a text in the Greek version of Isaiah 7.14.

Luke seems subtler in the way he places his account of the
virginal conception over against the OT background. He
looks back to various extraordinary conceptions in Jewish
history and to great persons born from the barren wombs of
older women. He evokes the story of Isaac and Jacob, who
were born to previously barren mothers (Luke 3.34). Even
more clearly, by echoing (Luke 1.46–55) the prayer of Hannah
(1 Samuel 2.1–10), a barren woman who late in life conceived

and gave birth to Samuel, a remarkable prophetic and priestly figure, Luke suggests how such births prefigured the virginal conception of Jesus. The evangelist does not take up Isaiah 7.14, which – unlike the OT texts about such older, barren women as Sarah (the mother of Isaac), Rebekah (the mother of Jacob) and Hannah – speaks of a young woman of marriageable age who is presumably fertile. Nor does Luke find any texts in the OT which speak of someone being conceived and born through the power of the Holy Spirit. The messianic king to come from the house of David will enjoy six gifts from the divine Spirit (Isaiah 11.1–2), but it is never said that he would be conceived by the Spirit.

The climactic example of a barren woman giving birth to some extraordinary son is reached with the promise of John the Baptist's conception (Luke 1.5–17). Clearly Luke sees nothing impure about married love and the normal way of conception; great joy follows the sexual union of the aged Zachariah and Elizabeth and the birth of their son (Luke 1.58). But Luke acknowledges a kind of quantum leap when the conception of Jesus brings a new, unexpected life from a young virgin.

In his two books, his Gospel and the Acts of the Apostles, Luke reports various miracles worked not only by Jesus but also by his followers – in particular, by Peter and Paul. Like Jesus, the apostles heal cripples, drive out demons, and even raise the dead (e.g. Acts 3.1–10; 5.14–16; 8.4–8; 9.32–43; 14.8–10). But Luke never claims that any of Jesus' followers ever brought about, through the power of the Holy Spirit, a virginal conception. Jesus' virginal conception stands apart, a special, even unique action of God that may not be repeated, as are the characteristic miracles worked by Jesus in his ministry (see Luke 7.22–3). Like his glorious resurrection from the dead, his virginal conception towers above the 'normal' miracles attributed to Jesus and his followers.

Matthew and Luke refer to the virginal conception from

different standpoints – Matthew from that of Joseph, Luke from that of Mary. The traditions on which they draw, the ways in which they develop them, and the OT language and motifs that they adapt for their infancy narratives differ markedly. We simply cannot harmonize into a unified account the opening chapters of the two Gospels. Nevertheless, Raymond Brown seems correct in holding that 'both Matthew and Luke regarded the virginal conception as historical'.[5] In other words, the two evangelists presented the conception of Jesus as actually taking place not through normal sexual intercourse but through a special intervention of the Holy Spirit. But what religious significance is conveyed by this unique manner of conception? What might be said if we follow the example of St Thomas Aquinas, who was not satisfied with merely upholding the fact of the virginal conception but wanted to show how it was 'appropriate' and religiously illuminating (ST 3a.28.1)?

The significance of the virginal conception

Traditionally the major value of the virginal conception has been to express Jesus' divine origin. The fact that he was born of a woman pointed to his humanity. The fact that he was conceived and born of a virgin pointed to his divinity and his eternal, personal origin as the Son of God. Jesus has a human mother but no (biological) human father – a startling sign of his divine generation by God the Father within the eternal life of God. *How* he came to be (and, subsequently, *how* he acted) revealed *who/what* he was and *from where* he had come.

The virginal conception also yields meaning about Jesus' relationship with the Holy Spirit. Christians experienced the outpouring of the Spirit in the aftermath of Jesus' resurrection from the dead. They came to appreciate how the Spirit, sent to them by the risen Christ or in his name, had been actively present in the whole of his life, not only at his baptism and through his subsequent ministry but also right back at his conception. In other words, the risen Jesus blessed his followers with the Spirit. But in his entire earthly existence he had been blessed by the Spirit – right from his very conception when he came into the world through the Spirit's creative power.

Thus the event of the virginal conception plays its part in revealing and clarifying that central truth: from the beginning to the end of Jesus' story, the Trinity is manifested. His total history discloses the God who is Father, Son and Holy Spirit.

As well as helping to reveal the tripersonal God, the virginal conception has something significant to say about human salvation. Christ's conception, by initiating the climactic phase of redemption or new creation, shows that salvation comes as divine gift. Human beings cannot inaugurate and carry through their own redemption. Like the original creation of the universe, the new creation is divine work and pure grace – to be received on the human side, just as Mary received the new life in her womb.

Notes

1. There are of course, sad to say, some Christians who reject both the incarnation and the virginal conception.
2. W. Pannenberg, *Jesus – God and Man* (London: SCM Press, 1968), 143, 146.
3. See H. Chadwick, *Origen, Contra Celsum*, 6.8 (Cambridge: Cambridge University Press, 1955), 321, n. 12.
4. R. E. Brown, *The Virginal Conception and Bodily Resurrection of Jesus* (London: Geoffrey Chapman, 1974), 64.
5. R. E. Brown, *The Birth of the Messiah*, new edition (New York: Doubleday, 1993), 517.

10

The Incarnation and Salvation

To you is born this day in the city of David a Saviour, who is Christ the Lord. And this will be a sign for you: you will find a baby wrapped in swaddling cloths and laid in a manger. (Luke 2.11–12)

He [the Christ Child] is wrapped in cloths but he clothes us with immortality. (Augustine of Hippo, *Sermons*, 190.4)

Many writers have described the human situation as an irredeemable mess. 'History', declared Voltaire, 'is no more than a tableau of crimes and misfortunes.'

Jonathan Glover, as powerfully as anyone, has presented the pitiless atrocities which characterized the twentieth century, that most violent century of human history.[1] Glover's troublingly accurate account could tempt one to write a premature epitaph for a world in which nationalistic fears and economic greed so often continue to disregard and ride roughshod over the basic rights of human beings and the well-being of our planet. In the competitive, capitalist 'culture' of Western society, success is *the* preoccupation and health the great dream. The indifferent and selfish masters of the world seem tragically shortsighted as they promote limitless economic growth, try to find military solutions for human problems, and 'oppress' the earth along with the men and women who populate it. Humanity seems to be dying on its feet, as it totters from one disaster to another.

In such a setting the crucified figure of Christ no longer exercises, even for many believers, the spell-binding attraction it once did. Much Western culture finds little meaning and purpose in suffering, and in fact often treats suffering and death as ugly taboos to be tidied away into hospitals and crematoria. The idea of ultimate deliverance coming through Jesus' crucifixion and resurrection seems preposterous. And yet liberal optimism and refined rationalism have lost much of their fresh appeal. It seems terribly irresponsible to gloss over the many personal and collective situations which put human existence into profound crisis.

The need for salvation

There is much to tell when we reflect on the forces of sin and evil which defile, imprison and prove deadly to human beings and their planet. The desire to establish and enjoy one's own autonomy, often a transparent mask for tragic hedonism, constantly turns sour and self-destructive. Brooding fears about health and death trap people in an anxious solitude. Sooner or later the ways in which we can choose to alienate ourselves from one another, from our earth, from God and from ourselves take us towards a kind of hell of absurdity which lacks genuine life and love.

An inherited solidarity in sin, which our personal sins express and endorse, finds abundant confirmation from human behaviour at the beginning of the third millennium. Such novels as *The Fall* by Albert Camus (1913–60) spell out our universal lack of innocence. The fictional works of Flannery O'Connor (1925–64) depict even more vividly the ubiquitous presence of sin and evil that goes back to human origins. Although offered their Creator's friendship, 'Adam and Eve' substitute themselves for God by independently deciding on good and evil and determining their destiny for themselves. Alienated from God, 'the man and his wife' become alienated from one another (Genesis 3.16) and find their world spiralling out of control into murder and vengeful violence (Genesis 4.24). 'Adam and Eve' symbolize not only the dignity of human beings made in the divine image and likeness (Genesis 1.26–7) but also their solidarity in sin from which the Redeemer comes to deliver them.

If we take a fresh look at biblical images of the human need for salvation, we can glimpse once again how they vividly characterize our condition. Adam and Eve experience their moral failure and find themselves to be naked; they need to be clothed and protected. Some chapters later in the book of Genesis, an avalanche of human sin corrupts the earth, which turns deadly in a cataclysmic flood. Later books of the OT tell of the sufferings of God's people when enslaved by Egypt and, later, when taken away to exile in Babylon. Slavery and exile continue to express poignantly the human experience of evil and sin. We are not free but dominated by deadly forces. We are forced (or let ourselves be forced) to live in a foreign place and not where we belong. The brutal suffering and killing of innumerable innocent human beings find their tragic expression in the torn and tortured body of the suffering servant (Isaiah 52.13–53.12). Evil and sin can plunge us into 'the depths' and 'pits' evoked by some of the Psalms (e.g. Psalm 130). We can feel ourselves to have been submerged and abandoned in subterranean darkness (Psalm 88). Nakedness, flood waters, slavery, exile, torture and the dark depths remain powerful symbols that help us to get to grips with the human need for salvation.

Salvation in a triple key

The Bible, texts for worship, and the whole Christian inheritance offer a rich variety of ways of reflecting on salvation or – what is its equivalent – redemption. These two terms have different roots but function more or less interchangeably. Despite the rich variety in language and imagery for salvation, a triple classification covers much of what is offered: love, victory and expiation.

First, we do not have to dig deeply into the Scriptures to establish that God's initiative of love clarifies the story of salvation. Sometimes this is put quite explicitly: 'God so loved the world that he gave his only Son' (John 3.16). Sometimes what is said remains unintelligible if that love is ignored. Thus Jesus' longest and most beautiful parable, which shows a father dealing so compassionately with the painful difficulties created by his two sons, never mentions love explicitly but transparently points to the divine love at work through Jesus (Luke 15.11–32). Other relationships, over and above that of parents/children, supply the NT with such salvific images as that of bridegroom/bride (e.g. Ephesians 5.25–7; Revelation 21.2, 9–10) and the teacher who wants to found a new family by turning his students into his brothers, sisters, and even his mother (Mark 3.35). None of these images for the redemptive process can be properly appreciated if we neglect the divine love revealed and at work in Christ. He is the high priest in loving solidarity with those he represents (Hebrews 4.15), the merciful doctor at table with the sinful sick (Mark 2.15–17), and the dedicated shepherd who knows all his sheep by name and is ready even to die for them (John 10.1–16).

Jesus' redemptive project promises to satisfy the human hunger for community and connection. We yearn to belong somewhere, to find a place of welcome and to live in loving relationship. Without love nothing would exist at all. In the beginning God showed infinite love by creating the universe and its centre, human beings. God's overflowing goodness gave birth and gives birth to everything that is. Divine love lay behind the original creation when God gave life to what had not yet existed. In the new creation initiated by Christ, God's love lifts us from the depths of darkness, clothes our nakedness, and gives us fresh life in a communion of love that will be perfected in the final home-coming of resurrection. It is no wonder that Jesus repeatedly pictures the goal of redemption as a joyful banquet that will never end, a feast of love when all will rejoice together in the kingdom of God (e.g. Matthew 8.11).

Second, from the beginning of Christianity, the theme of victorious conflict established itself as a second major key for interpreting salvation. This was hardly surprising, since Christ's death and resurrection took place during the days when Jews celebrated their exodus from Egypt, God's delivering them from slavery to freedom. During his ministry Jesus himself had already presented his activity as his victorious conflict with satanic powers (Mark 3.27). In the post-Easter situation various NT authors followed suit by expounding Christ's salvific work as bringing deliverance from the forces of evil: sin, death and diabolic powers. The manumission of slaves and the ransoming of prisoners of war also helped to shape the cultural setting in which NT Christians proclaimed Christ as 'redeeming', 'buying', 'ransoming' or 'liberating' sinful men and women. The act of redemption was 'costly', in the sense that it cost Christ his life and not in the sense of his paying a price to God, let alone the devil, to set us free. This language centred on Christ effecting our deliverance from the forces which oppress us.

The NT already shows a sense of the paradoxical nature of this triumph: for instance, in its language about the 'victory' of the Lamb 'who was slain' (Revelation 5.6–14). The post-NT Church cherished the theme of Christ's redemptive victory and its surprisingly paradoxical nature. St Augustine of Hippo (d. 430) declared: 'slain by death, he slew death' (*In Joannem*, 12.10–11). The classical hymns of Venantius Fortunatus (d. *c.* 610) and even more the Easter sequence of Wipo (d. after 1046), 'To the Easter victim (*Victimae paschali*)', celebrated Christ's salvific battle, that 'marvellous duel in which death and life fought'. In the Anglo-Saxon poem 'The Dream of the Rood' and other medieval religious poetry, Christ appeared as the heroic warrior who fell in seeming defeat but whose courage in fact carried the day.

To celebrate this deliverance, Christian worship has pressed into service the songs with which Moses and Miriam led the people in praising God for their victorious liberation from slavery in Egypt (Exodus 15.1–21). While the exodus story remained the prototype *par excellence* of such redemptive deliverance, Christian writers and artists from the earliest times found other precedents in such OT stories as Noah and his family being rescued from the flood, Daniel from the lions' den, the three youths from the fiery furnace, Jonah from the great fish and Susannah from the two wicked elders. For many Christians the image of redemption as victory stays vividly alive in the *Exultet* or Easter Proclamation, sung every Holy Saturday night: 'This is the night in which Christ, breaking the bonds of death, rose victorious from the tomb.'

A third version of redemption is built around Christ as the priest and victim who, through the last supper, his passion, the crucifixion and the resurrection, offers once and for all as our representative the sacrifice which expiates sin and brings a new covenantal relationship between God and the human race. Such expiation presupposes that human beings are defiled by sin and in need of cleansing. The Suffering Servant of Isaiah 53 prefigured the cruel sufferings of the innocent Christ, whose suffering expiates the sins of others.

It was not that the atrocious suffering which Christ underwent simply had value in and of itself. Being tortured to death just as such redeems no one. The issue changes, however, since it was loving and obedient self-giving which put Christ into the hands of his killers. His total innocence and his divine identity gave unique value to his self-sacrifice. By raising him from the dead and glorifying him, God accepted and 'made holy' the victim and high priest, who thus entered into the heavenly sanctuary (Hebrews 8.2; 9.24). This 'powerful' dealing with sin and its terrible consequences for human beings and their world occurred, paradoxically, through the 'weakness' of love, the love which accepted the cross. Self-giving love prevailed over the worst of human malice and rehabilitated sinful humanity.

Salvation and incarnation

Some readers may accept, more or less cheerfully, this three-fold way of reading what Christ did and does to save a sick and sinful world. But they could well object that this reading encompasses an extended narrative: from Christ's conception through to his final coming, with special emphasis on the events of the first Good Friday and Easter Sunday. In other words, the redemptive impact of the incarnation comes through, only if we follow Chapter 3 above and take 'incarnation' in the broader sense of the whole story of God's special action in and through Christ 'for us and for our salvation', as the creeds put it.

Nevertheless, Christian prayers, hymns and works of art have repeatedly understood the very conception and birth of Jesus to bring salvation to the world. Two verses of a traditional Sussex carol find the fruits of redemption in the celebration of Christmas:

Then why should men on earth be so sad,
Since our Redeemer made us glad,
When from our sin he set us free,
All for to gain our liberty?

When sin departs before his grace,
Then life and health come in its place;
Angels and men with joy may sing,
All for to see the new-born King.

Right in the setting of Christ's birth this carol rejoices over some of the major aspects of redemption, which St Paul highlights in Romans 8 and other chapters of his masterpiece: redemption as freedom 'from the law of sin and death', as abounding grace, health and life, and as the joy of those who can pray and sing together in the solidarity of God's adopted sons and daughters. The carol suggests applying to the conception and birth of Jesus the threefold scheme outlined above.

First, by our very nature as interlocking human beings, we long to be loved and to love – to be bonded with one another and with God. At the coming of Jesus, divine actions speak louder than words – even before any words can be uttered by the incarnate Son of God. The birth of Jesus shows us how God loves us extravagantly; we are all utterly precious in the eyes of God. By recognizing the Christ Child to be the personal presence of the incarnate Word, believers know how much God values and cherishes them. The divine identity of that baby reveals what we mean and meant to God. The alternative, a Jesus who is not truly divine, implies that God was unwilling to assume our human condition and did not and does not, after all, set such a high value on us.

Seen in this way, the birth of Jesus is the effective presence and manifestation of God's love for us. Just as God did not need to create a universe, so God did not need to be incarnated. Other ways could have been found to deal with the mess caused by human sin. But the boundlessly loving God, who at the beginning of the story of the universe chose to bring all things into existence, now wants to share personally in the life of human beings and bring them a glorious future in the new creation.

From the second century many Christian writers highlighted 'the wonderful exchange (*admirabile commercium*)', through which the Son of God became human so that we humans might become 'divine': that is to say, so that we might share through grace in the very life of God. This key to the whole story of saving exchange remains unintelligible if we leave out God's love, the infinitely generous desire to bring us into the communion of ecstatic love which is the eternal life of the Trinity. Significantly the divine office closely associates this *admirabile commercium* with the birth of Jesus by using it for the opening antiphon for the first and second vespers of 1 January, the octave day of Christmas: 'O wonderful exchange! The Creator of human nature took on a human body and was born of the Virgin. He became man without having a human father and has bestowed on us his divine nature.'

Second, the victorious impact of the incarnation began with the conception and birth of Christ. The interlocking of all people and all things means that the personal and physical presence of the Son of God changed at once the whole material world. Something dramatically new happened. A divine Being was now physically and personally present among and in relation with all other beings. Right from the birth in Bethlehem, we could see, hear and touch God (1 John 1.1). In the third millennium we are more than ever aware of the many ways in which everything and everyone were and are inter-related and interdependent. That awareness allows believers to acknowledge how through the newborn Jesus a radical change took place for humanity and the cosmos. One did not have to wait for his death and resurrection to initiate such a salvific impact on a world groaning for redemption (Romans 8.18–25). With the very coming of Christ, the victory over the powers that alienate and destroy had already begun.

Matthew's story of the visit of the Magi and its aftermath shows how God's power is already at work to overcome evil (Matthew 2.1–18). When a vicious and cunning king, Herod the Great, learns of the birth of the 'King of the Jews', he tries to trick the wise men into betraying the whereabouts of the Christ Child. But through a dream and an angel, respectively, God allows the Magi and the Holy Family to escape from all harm. Herod represents the powerful and violent forces of evil which line up against seemingly 'weak' persons, who are led by the Christ Child in working for the salvation of the world. What is a baby, his parents and several foreign visitors against the might of a great king? But God effortlessly acts to frustrate evil plots and rescue the Holy Family and the Magi. The whole story suggests the divine power at its saving work in what seems a situation of desperate human weakness.

Third, as regards the third key to the drama of redemption, Christ's sacrifice of expiation, Christian painters (in depicting the visit of the shepherds and the circumcision) have left little doubt that events surrounding his birth set that sacrifice going. Like other Jewish male infants, the Christ Child was circumcised eight days after his birth. The ritual removal of his foreskin recalled and symbolized God's covenant with Abraham (Genesis 17.11–12) and remained part of the religious practice maintained by Moses (Leviticus 12.3). Circumcision marked, as well, the moment when a male child was formally named.

The name of 'Jesus' given to Mary's child was popularly understood to mean 'Saviour' or 'God saves'; strictly speaking, it meant 'Lord, help!' Either way, the name given to the Christ Child connected him very directly to the work of salvation, which would reach its climax with his sacrificial death on the cross. Christian theologians and artists drew further significance from the slight loss of blood entailed by circumcision, seeing in this an anticipation of the passion and death through which Christ would expiate the sins of the world.

Painters also exploited the visit of the shepherds (Luke 2.20) and of the Magi (Matthew 2.1–12) to the newborn Jesus as episodes which intimated and prepared for the expiatory sacrifice to come. To Luke's story of the shepherds' visit, painters often added some sheep and, occasionally, a bound lamb – a very clear reference to Christ's dying as the Lamb of God who takes away the sin of the world (John 1.29). The Spanish artist Francisco de Zurbarán (1598–1664) concentrated on this image of Christ's sacrifice by painting several times a young lamb, its feet bound, and lying on a stone slab which is set against a dark and menacing background.

The Magi in Matthew's story bring the Christ Child several gifts, one of which is myrrh, traditionally associated with death and embalming. As we saw in Chapter 3, some artists exploited this gift of myrrh to link the birth of Jesus with his sacrificial death and burial.

Two conclusions

In Matthew's Gospel the Magi form one of the first links in a whole chain of episodes and sayings through which the text will allude to the universal significance of the salvation Jesus is bringing. These exotic strangers from the East symbolize that salvation is for everyone and every culture. Some final words from the risen Jesus will make the worldwide impact of his redemptive mission utterly clear (Matthew 28.19–20). But through the Magi Matthew has already shown how Christ at his birth is already the Saviour of all people. By tracing Christ's descent from Adam (Luke 3.38), Luke's Gospel also early on hints at the universal impact of the sal-

vation Christ will effect. The Son of Mary will prove himself
the new head for the entire human race. Already known to be
the Saviour at his birth (Luke 2.11), Jesus will bring about
personally and with his Holy Spirit the return of all people to
God in the glory of the final kingdom.

Matthew and Luke also show how the blessing of redemption turns the men and women blessed by Christ into
secondary agents of redemption. Luke's opening chapters, in
particular, surround the birth of Jesus with older and
younger men and women, who all have crucial roles to play in
the unfolding drama of salvation. The gift of redemption
becomes a responsibility.[2]

Thus far I have tackled the incarnation from various
angles: biblical, theological, artistic and philosophical. What
remains is perhaps the most daunting task: why and how can
one accept the incarnation? What is to be said about its
credibility?

Notes

1. *Humanity. A Moral History of the Twentieth Century* (New Haven
    and London: Yale University Press, 1999).
2. For further material on redemption and the incarnation, see
    'Atonement', 'Redemption', 'Sacrifice' and 'Salvation' in A. Hastings
    et al. (eds), *The Oxford Companion to Christian Thought* (Oxford:
    Oxford University Press, 2000).

The Credibility of the Incarnation

These things are written that you may believe that
Jesus is the Christ, the Son of God, and that believing
you may have life in his name. (John 20.31)

> And is it true? And is it true?
> This most tremendous tale of all . . .
> The Maker of the stars and sea
> Became a Child on earth for me?
> (Sir John Betjeman, 'Christmas')

The aim of John's Gospel was to encourage faith in the incarnate Son of God, since that faith would bring life for ever and
in abundance. Yet such faith in Jesus as truly divine is startling. During the Mass he attended at Christmas 1986, the
American novelist Walker Percy was deeply surprised by a
powerful religious experience. He wrote about it at once to
Robert Coles, a psychiatrist friend at Harvard University:

Dear Bob, The Mass was going on, the homily standard
– that is 'true' but customary. A not-so-good choir of
young rock musicians got going on 'Joy to the World',
the vocals not so good but enthusiastic. Then it hit me:
What if it should be the case that the entire cosmos had
a Creator, and what if he decided for reasons of his own

to show up as a tiny baby, conceived and born under suspicious circumstances?

'Well, Bob,' Walker Percy continued, 'you can lay it on Alzheimer's or hang-over or whatever, but – it hit me. I had to pretend I had an allergy attack so that I could take out my handkerchief.'

Walker Percy was always an intellectual, tightly controlled man, who had never had anything close to a mystical experience or even a twinge of pentecostal enthusiasm. The experience he wrote about came late in his life, that sense of stunned amazement at the divine Word becoming flesh and living among us. Despite his Southern reserve, Percy was profoundly astonished and wept at the sheer loving simplicity of what God had done at the first Christmas.

But why should we share Percy's faith and join Sir John Betjeman in agreeing that 'the Maker of the stars and sea' really did become 'a Child on earth for me'? One's 'background' theory about God and our human condition can be decisive here.

Background theory

Views about God and human possibilities can make or break faith in the incarnation. In his dialogue with Trypho, St Justin Martyr (d. *c.* 165) found that this Jewish thinker dismissed the incarnation as incredible and impossible. Being unchanging and so far beyond our world of space and time, God could not assume our mutable human condition, be born among us, and then die on a cross. A few years later Celsus, a learned pagan philosopher who admired much of the ethical teaching of Christianity, similarly dismissed the very possibility of the Word assuming the human condition. Two centuries further on, St Augustine wrote of the Platonic philosophers that they could accept the Word being generated eternally by God, but not that the Word might become flesh (*Confessions*, 7.9).

Where Platonic-style philosophers ruled out in principle the incarnation by separating God as pure spirit from the material world, Stoics rejected the incarnation for opposite reasons. Like other pantheists, Stoics believed that God was already 'within' the material world and immanent in everything. If that is so, the Son of God could not take on a material, human condition and enter the created universe. The divinity is already universally present, being identical with everything.

But other philosophical currents gave incarnation faith a certain plausibility. Dionysius the Pseudo-Areopagite (*c.* 500), a mystical writer who combined Platonic themes with Christianity, defended the notion of 'the good' by its very nature 'disseminating or sharing itself (*honum diffusivum sui*)'. Such a notion leads on to thinking that the good and loving self-communication manifested in creation might prompt God into a further act of self-sharing by the personal self-giving that was the incarnation.

Views about the human condition and its possibilities can also prove decisive in supporting faith in the incarnation. Those who acknowledge the dynamism of the human spirit and its openness to the infinite will find a certain plausibility in the idea of a limit case in human possibilities: God's Son has assumed and 'personalized' one particular, created human being, Jesus of Nazareth. Here is the limit case for humanity in its dynamic openness to the infinite God, as the fullness of all being and of all goodness.

In short, prior views about God, humanity and its inherent possibilities can close or open people to belief in the incarnation. But what kind of case might justify such a belief, or at least give it a certain plausibility?

An incarnation apologetic

Any apologetic needs to be shaped by its audience, and audiences can vary a great deal. They may come from those who follow non-Christian religions, from Christians who have begun to seriously question the truth of the incarnation, or from those who profess to having no religious faith at all. The educational qualifications of one's audience may run all the way from children in primary schools to candidates for doctorates. The setting in which one develops a reasonable case for faith in the incarnation can be a school, a parish, a hospital, a gaol, a radio station, or the economy cabin of a jumbo-jet flying the Atlantic.

That said, some coherence, pragmatic considerations and correspondence with the data will normally affect the case being developed. Let me explain. First, we would normally expect such a startling belief as the incarnation of the pre-existent Son of God to cohere in some way with what we otherwise know and accept about reality, above all about the ultimate reality of God and ourselves. To present this belief as totally new would be to present something utterly incomprehensible. In some way it needs to 'fit into' what we already know; otherwise neither we nor anyone else could make any sense of it. Here Justin's dialogue with Trypho proves illuminating. In his apologetic for Christ, his divinity and his incarnation, Justin drew on the Hebrew Scriptures, sacred texts accepted both by himself and by his Jewish interlocutor. The challenge for Justin was to show how his new, Christian faith cohered, at least partially, with what they both accepted in faith about God and the human condition.

To some extent this first test of coherence coincides with what is credible to our imagination. Some people fear that appeals to the imagination will lead us astray, but many follow the dictum of John Keats (d. 1821): 'What the imagination seizes as beautiful must be truth.' Our imagination yearns for a total, coherent picture of things, and is fired by the radiant harmony of what is beautiful. Does belief in the incarnation come across as beautiful, something which can harmoniously order our view of reality?

In a remarkable testimony to the unique beauty of Christ, our divine 'spouse', St Augustine declared him to be 'beautiful in the womb of the Virgin', beautiful 'when he sucked [his mother's] milk', beautiful 'when he was carried in the arms of his parents'. Augustine took a proper, full view of the incarnation and went on to say: 'he was beautiful in his miracles, beautiful in his sufferings, beautiful in inviting to life, beautiful in not being worried about death, beautiful in laying down his life, beautiful in taking it up again, beautiful on the cross, beautiful in the tomb, beautiful in heaven'. Augustine recognized 'the splendour' of Christ's beauty deployed at all points of the incarnation, even in the hideous suffering of the cross (*Ennarationes in Psalmos*, 44.3).

In earlier chapters we have, from time to time, cited the testimony of outstanding poets, musicians and painters – geniuses who stood out for their sensitive appreciation of the beauty they glimpsed in the incarnate Son of God. The incarnation fired their imagination and engaged their energies. We might sum up their conviction as 'the incarnation is too beautiful not to be true'. One of the greatest witnesses to the beauty of the incarnate Son of God has to be Rembrandt Harmensz van Rijn (d. 1669). Significantly, this supreme artist followed Augustine in drawing attention to the divine beauty of Christ manifested not only in his life and resurrection but also in his suffering and crucifixion. Rembrandt was second to none in capturing the haunting beauty of Christ in his passion.

Second, the incarnation needs to be tested 'pragmatically': that is to say, by scrutinizing the practical consequences of incarnation faith. Has this faith transformed the lives of believers, by leading to good or even remarkable results in their behaviour towards other human beings and towards

God? Has accepting the truth of the incarnation shown its practical efficacy in positive ways that meet with widespread, if not universal, approval? Undoubtedly a fully informed response to such questions calls for an expert grasp of human and Christian history. Nevertheless, one might undertake such a 'social confirmation' of incarnation faith by reflecting on the behaviour of contemporary believers and facing the question: can generous, even heroic, service of the suffering continue to be motivated by false beliefs about God and the divine presence in our world? 'Incarnation House' in New York provides one striking example: the very name of the institution signals the faith which inspires believers, including many younger ones, to lavish care on babies whose life expectancy is limited since they have been born HIV-positive.

Correspondence with the available data constitutes a third test for incarnation faith. This scrutiny will assume a largely historical form. What can be verified about Jesus' life, death and resurrection that could support those who accept him as the incarnate Son of God? What did he, at least implicitly, claim about his own identity and authority? How convincing is the vision of God which pervaded Jesus' preaching of the kingdom? Were the behaviour and moral perfection of Jesus such as one might expect from the Son of God incarnate? What does the evidence for his intimacy with God say about his identity? In the aftermath of his death and resurrection, together with the outpouring of the Holy Spirit, Jesus' followers came to confess him as their divine Lord and the Son of God sent among them. Does their testimony encourage us to join them in that appreciation of his identity and function?

In the twentieth century G. K. Chesterton (d. 1936) and, even more clearly, C. S. Lewis (d. 1963) developed a 'bad', 'mad' or '(Son of) God' argument. The claims Jesus made to an authority that has to be acknowledged as divine leaves us with three possibilities: he was morally and religiously wicked; or he was out of his mind; or his claims were true and he genuinely was the Son of God come among us. At the end of the first century AD, John's Gospel presents a similar choice in Jesus' controversy with his critics: either Jesus is a 'liar', or he is unbalanced and 'has a demon', or else he is truly the divine 'Light of the world' (John 8.13–52). Not too many critics of Jesus have dismissed him as morally and religiously bad. But a few, such as the British writer and sexologist Henry Havelock Ellis (d. 1939), have argued that Jesus was a candidate for a lunatic asylum. In his *Impressions and Comments* Ellis complained that there was no such lunatic asylum in the suburbs of ancient Jerusalem: otherwise Jesus 'would infallibly have been shut up in it at the outset of his public career'. The most controversial element in this 'mad, bad or Son of God' argument is undoubtedly its point of departure. Can we verify that Jesus, at least by implication, claimed an authority and identity that were truly divine?[1]

Such then are three tests with which incarnation faith could be scrutinized. Does it yield a coherent picture of ultimate reality? What are its results in practice? Does it correspond to the data we can verify about Jesus? Those who reach a positive conclusion here are, in effect, declaring the incarnation to be beautiful, good and true. We need all three tests, since one of them alone might lead us astray. The history of cosmology and science, for instance, yields many examples of imaginable constructs that have subsequently been proved to be false.

Grace and God

No appeal to the kind of cumulative argument proposed above should mask the fact that all authentic faith, and not least explicit faith in the incarnate Son of God, emerges and endures only through the gracious help of God. The external witness of Christian artists, believers and scholars always

needs to be supported by the interior help from the Holy
Spirit. Without that help, no external testimony will bring
real faith in Jesus Christ. A rational case can be constructed
in support of the incarnation, but faith is the gift of God and
never simply the conclusion of a merely human argument.
God's gifts now can seem as mysterious as God's past
choices in biblical history. Why did God choose the Jewish
people for a special destiny and not, for instance, the people of
ancient China? Why was the Son of God born 2,000 years ago
in Palestine and not earlier, later or somewhere else? From
the early centuries of Christianity and later, some writers
have found reasons for such divine choices. Providence and
the peace of the emerging Roman Empire provided the right
setting for the birth of Jesus in the east of the Mediterranean
world. But one could well argue that certain periods in the
history of ancient India or China, for example, could also
have been appropriate contexts for the incarnation.

The history of divine choices in the OT history repeatedly
contains surprises. Over and over again God picks out less
promising candidates, like younger sons and barren women,
for special vocations. God's call goes out to some prophets
such as Ezechiel whose personality problems (or should we
describe them as 'disorders'?) seem to disqualify them for
major roles in the history of salvation. Whatever else we
learn from the story of God's people, at least we should reach
the conclusion: God's ways and choices are not our ways and
choices. Or we might endorse the old proverb, 'God writes
straight with crooked lines.'

Even if in retrospect we can spot some meaning in the
timing, place and other circumstances for the incarnation, we
will do better by joining the martyred bishop, St Ignatius of
Antioch, in respecting reverently the mystery and 'silence' of
God that characterizes the birth of the Son of God (*To the
Ephesians*, 19). A silent, even tearful wonder may well be our
most appropriate reaction to the incarnation.

Note

1. See S. T. Davis, 'Was Jesus Mad, Bad, or God?', in S. T. Davis, D. Kendall and G. O'Collins (eds), *The Incarnation* (Oxford: Oxford University Press, 2002), 221–45.

12

Concluding Evaluations

May the Lord bless you and guard you; may the Lord
make his face shine on you and be gracious to you; may
the Lord look kindly on you and give you peace.
(Numbers 6.24–6)

History is a nightmare from which I am trying to
awake. (James Joyce, *Ulysses*)

Self-evaluation is notoriously a questionable business, at
least when it results in self-congratulatory judgements. But
perhaps critical self-evaluation can be more useful and illuminating. Looking over all the previous chapters, I think four
themes deserve more attention.

First, Eastern icons and other images seem to me more
instructive than ever. The fact that a cave rather than a stall
for cattle provides the central focus for Eastern icons of the
nativity links very effectively the event of the incarnation
with what is to follow: in particular, at the death and burial of
Jesus. These icons regularly place the Child Jesus in a tomb
– a powerful way of indicating that his birth and death reveal
his extravagant love for us. St Paul knows that the incarnation is fundamentally sacrificial and concerned with God's
self-sacrificing, redeeming love (Romans 8.1–4). What the
apostle expresses in theological prose finds its visual counterpart in holy images of Eastern Christianity.

As we also saw in Chapter 3, the way Western Christians in the Middle Ages brought together the creation of the world, the incarnation and human redemption was encouraged by the fact that very occasionally Good Friday occurred on the date for the Feast of the Annunciation, 25 March. Between the years 1000 and 1500 this happened thirteen times. It might prove illuminating to trace and examine images and sermons composed for those occasions.

A second theme which could be further developed is the paradoxical character of the incarnation in being both astonishingly new and also, in a sense, almost what one might expect from God. That one and the same person could be simultaneously truly divine and fully human is something beyond anything that even great thinkers like Aristotle and Confucius ever thought of and took to be possible. Nevertheless, even though belief in the incarnation involves something extraordinarily new, utterly surprising and contrary to human expectations, Christians who reflect on the tender closeness of God celebrated by Hosea, Isaiah, Jeremiah and other great prophets, can feel like saying: 'That the Word became flesh seems all of a piece with the loving closeness of God to his people.'

Third, the celebration of the incarnation in public worship invited more attention than it received. A remarkable and much-neglected passage from the Second Vatican Council's Constitution on the Sacred Liturgy has linked the incarnation with praising God and praying for the salvation of the entire world:

> By assuming a human nature, Jesus Christ, the High Priest of the new and eternal covenant, introduced into this earthly exile that hymn which is sung through all ages in the halls of heaven. He unites to himself the entire human community, and associates them with himself in singing this divine song of praise. (*Sacrosanctum Concilium*, 83)

The redemptive work of Christ has often been understood in terms of his priestly, prophetic and kingly role. This passage, coming as it does from a document on the liturgy, naturally highlights the priestly 'office' of Christ. His incarnation reveals him as *the* eternal priest – not only for the new family of the Church but also for the entire human community. His saving work for all men and women of all places and times inseparably follows from his assuming our common human condition. By picturing redemption as singing together with the incarnate Christ an eternal, heavenly hymn to God, the Council associates the incarnation with the redemption in a cosmic praise of God which joins together those who still endure 'this earthly exile' and those already enjoying the heavenly vision of God. So far from being a nightmare from which we yearn to wake, human history initiates an eternal chorus of loving praise to God.

Any radical hope for humanity rests finally on the Son of God's incarnation, a theme which should bulk larger in sermons which at Christmas and at other times address the incarnation. This fourth theme, of preaching the incarnation, might have enjoyed a chapter in this book. Here and always, theology should serve not only prayer but also public preaching. The passing parade on warm autumn evenings in Rome often makes me think of what Shakespeare wrote in *Cymbeline*: 'Golden lads and girls all must/As chimney sweepers come to dust.' The passage of time will take away the gloriously beautiful Italian youth, along with everyone and everything. But the birth of Christ means that eternity has come among us. The Eternal One rescues us from devouring time. We are not melancholy victims of our history but candidates for eternity, a sacred family moving towards its final home and not a herd of lemmings destined for destruction.

Whatever else I may have achieved in this book, I hope it fuels some Christmas sermons and the well-founded conviction that the incarnation has brought for ever an astounding reversal in what human beings left to themselves might otherwise expect – or (should we say?) dread. The tiny Baby in Mary's arms has made the ancient Jewish blessing come true; the Lord's face is shining upon us. We are and will be blessed and guarded, because we can now see the divine glory on the face of the Christ Child.

A Select Bibliography

R. E. Brown, *The Birth of the Messiah*, new edition (London: Doubleday, 1993).

S. T. Davis, D. Kendall and G. O'Collins (eds), *The Incarnation* (Oxford: Oxford University Press, 2002).

C. S. Evans, *The Historical Christ and the Jesus of Faith: The Incarnational Narrative as History* (Oxford: Clarendon, 1996).

A. Grillmeier, *Christ in Christian Tradition*, 2 vols (London: Mowbrays, 1975–95).

P. van Inwagen, 'Incarnation and Christology', in *Routledge Encyclopedia of Philosophy*, vol. 4 (London: Routledge, 1998), 725–32.

T. V. Morris, *The Logic of God Incarnate* (Ithaca, NY: Cornell University Press, 1986).

R. Sturch, *The Word and the Christ* (Oxford: Clarendon Press, 1991).

NB Dictionaries and encyclopedias of Christian theology and history, as well as of religious studies, normally carry informative entries under 'Incarnation'.

Index of Names